The Report of the International Commission

for Central American Recovery and Development

Poverty, Conflict, and Hope

D1214254

The Report of the International Commission

for Central American Recovery and Development

Poverty, Conflict, and Hope

A Turning Point in Central America

Duke University Press   Durham and London 1989

338.9728
I 61 p
1989

© 1989 Duke University Press
Printed in the United States of America
on acid-free paper ∞
Library of Congress Cataloging-in-Publication Data
appear on the last printed page
of this book.

Contents

METHODIST COLLEGE LIBRARY
FAYETTEVILLE, NC

Members of the International Commission for
Central American Recovery and Development   (ICCARD)

Arthur Levitt, Jr., Co-Chair
(United States)
Chairman and Chief Executive
Officer, American Stock Exchange

Sonia Picado, Co-Chair (Costa Rica)
Executive Director, Inter-American
Institute of Human Rights
Judge, Inter-American Court
of Human Rights

Irma Acosta de Fortín (Honduras)
Rector and Founder,
Universidad José Cecilio Del Valle

Juan Francisco Alfaro (Guatemala)
General Secretary, Guatemalan
Confederation for Labor Unity
(CVSG)

Rodrigo Botero (Colombia)
Editor, Estrategia; Former
Colombian Minister of Finance

Guillermo Bueso (Honduras)
Executive Vice President and
General Manager, Banco Atlantida;

Director, Central Bank of Honduras;
Advisor, External Debt Negotiation
Commission

Pedro Abelardo Delgado
(El Salvador)
Advisor, Pan American Development
Foundation; President, New
Generation Financial Corporation;
Former President, Central Bank of
El Salvador

Claude Cheysson (France)
Former Commissioner for
Mediterranean Policies and
North-South Relations,
Commission of the European
Community

Juan José del Pino (Venezuela)
Secretary General,
Federation of Venezuelan Workers

Enrique Dreyfus (Nicaragua)
Honorary Chairman of the
Nicaraguan Private Sector Council
(COSEP); Chairman, Commission

on the Recovery and Development of Nicaragua (CORDENIC)

William M. Dyal, Jr. (United States)
President, St. John's College;
Founding President,
Inter-American Foundation

Lawrence S. Eagleburger
(United States)
President, Kissinger Associates, Inc.;
Former Undersecretary of State
for Political Affairs (Resigned in
January 1989 upon appointment as
Deputy Secretary of State.)

Richard E. Feinberg (United States)
Vice President,
Overseas Development Council

Albert Fishlow (United States)
Chairman, Department of
Economics, University of California
at Berkeley

Xabier Gorostiaga (Nicaragua)
Director, Regional Council for
Economic and Social Research
(CRIES)

Wolf Grabendorff (West Germany)
Founding Director, Institute for
European-Latin American Affairs
(IRELA)

Francisco de Paula Gutiérrez
(Costa Rica)
Director, Graduate Program in
Economics, Central American

Institute for Business
Management (INCAE)

Arnold Harberger (United States)
Director, Center for Latin American
Studies, University of Chicago;
Director, Program in Latin American
Economic Research, University of
California at Los Angeles

Alfred Hernández Contreras
(Guatemala)
General Manager, Guatemalan
Federation of Coffee-Producing
Cooperatives (FEDECOCAGUA)

David Ibarra (Mexico)
Consultant to PEMEX and the
United Nations; Former Minister of
Finance for Mexico

Glenn P. Jenkins (Canada)
Institute Fellow, Harvard Institute
for International Development

John T. Joyce (United States)
President, International Union of
Bricklayers and Allied Craftsmen

Yuzo Kamo (Japan)
Professor of History,
Aoyama Gakuin University, Tokyo

Walther Leisler Kiep (West Germany)
Former Member of the
West German Bundestag

Mikio Kojima (Japan)
President, Japan External Trade
Organization—New York

Pedro-Pablo Kuczynski (Peru)
Chairman, First Boston International

José Federico Linares Martínez
(Guatemala)
Managing Director, FIASA;
Former President, Central Bank and
Monetary Fund of Guatemala

Sol M. Linowitz (United States)
Senior Partner, Coudert Brothers;
Former U.S. Ambassador to the
Organization of American States

Carlyle Guerra de Macedo (Brazil)
Director,
Pan-American Health Organization
Juan Ramón Martínez (Honduras)
President, Federation of Honduran
Development Organizations

Francisco J. Mayorga (Nicaragua)
Director of Graduate Studies,
Central American Institute for
Business Management, Managua
(INCAE)

Arturo Morales-Carrión
(Puerto Rico)
Executive Director, Puerto Rican
Endowment for the Humanities

Roberto Murray-Meza (El Salvador)
President, La Constancia, S.A.;
Former President, Federation of
Private Enterprise Councils of
Central America and Panama
(FEDEPRICAP), and Salvadoran
Foundation for Economic and Social
Development (FUSADES)

Orlando Nuñez (Nicaragua)
Director, Center for the Study of
Agrarian Reform

Daniel Oduber (Costa Rica)
Former President of Costa Rica

Martín Piñeiro (Argentina)
Director General, Inter-American
Institute for Cooperation on
Agriculture (IICA)

Abraham Rodríguez (El Salvador)
First Designate to the Presidency of
El Salvador; Former Director,
Salvadoran Foundation for Economic
and Social Development (FUSADES)

Gert Rosenthal (Guatemala)
Executive Secretary,
United Nations Economic
Commission for Latin America
and the Caribbean (ECLAC)

Pierre Schori (Sweden)
Undersecretary of State,
Swedish Ministry for Foreign Affairs

Jesús Silva-Herzog (Mexico)
Former Minister of Finance
for Mexico

Ricardo Stein (Guatemala)
Former Director, Salvadoran
Foundation for Development and
Housing (FUNDASAL)

Peter Tarnoff (United States)
President, Council on
Foreign Relations

Edelberto Torres-Rivas (Guatemala)
Secretary General, Latin American
Faculty of Social Sciences (FLACSO)

Constantino Urcuyo (Costa Rica)
Economist, Center for Research and
Training in Public Administration
(CIAPA), Political Scientist,
University of Costa Rica

Viron P. Vaky (United States)
Senior Fellow, Carnegie
Endowment for International Peace;
Former Assistant Secretary of State
for Inter-American Affairs

Luis Yáñez-Barnuevo García (Spain)
Secretary of State for International
Cooperation, Spanish Ministry of
Foreign Affairs; President, Institute
for Iberoamerican Cooperation (ICI)

Sally W. Yudelman (United States)
Senior Fellow, International Center
for Research on Women; Former
Vice President for Programs,
Inter-American Foundation

Acknowledgments

The work of the International Commission for Central American Recovery and Development relied heavily on the advice and guidance of literally hundreds of people—from economists to translators, editors, and many other professionals. While it is not possible to acknowledge each individual, we express our sincere gratitude to all those who made our efforts a success.

The Commission would particularly like to thank those who served as special consultants to the Commission: Gordon Stewart, vice-president of the American Stock Exchange, and Joseph Thompson of the Interamerican Institute of Human Rights, as well as Mark Schneider, Joel Freedman, Hans Allden, Carmelo Angulo, Ricardo Gomez, Carlos Gutierrez, Lisa Lederer, and Jorge Werthein.

Organizations and government agencies in Latin America, North America, and Europe offered valuable consultation and guidance. We look forward to continued cooperation with the Central American Bank of Economic Integration, the U.S. Agency for International Development, the Inter-American Development Bank, the International Monetary Fund, the Permanent Secretariat for Central American Economic Integration (SIECA), the United Nations Development Programme, the World Bank, and governments and embassies in Central America and throughout the world. We also received valuable advice from a host of nongovernmental organizations, which played an important role in the development of our recommendations.

For their judgment and counsel, we are grateful to Marc Lindenberg of the John F. Kennedy School of Government, Isaac Cohen of ECLAC, Steven R. Brown of Kent State University, Geoff Pyatt of the Inter-American Dialogue, and several staff members of the U.S. Congress: Bill Green and Barbara Larkin of Senator Terry Sanford's office; Richard McCall of Senator John

Kerry's staff; and Andrew Semmel of Senator Richard Lugar's office.

The foundations who have supported us have provided both financial assistance and valuable advice. We wish to thank Smith Bagley, Margery Tabankin, and Janet Shenk of the Arca Foundation; Bill Bondurant of the Mary Reynolds Babcock Foundation; David Hamburg, Barbara Finberg, and Geraldine Mannion of the Carnegie Corporation of New York; Steve Cox and Stanley Heginbotham of the Ford Foundation; Ruth Adams of the John D. and Catherine T. MacArthur Foundation; and Peter Goldmark and Kenneth Prewitt of the Rockefeller Foundation.

We are also grateful to the government of Costa Rica for helping to facilitate our initial meeting, and to the Swedish Foreign Ministry and the Swedish International Development Authority, which served as excellent hosts for the June 1988 Commission meeting. Particularly helpful for the Stockholm meeting were Gabriella Lindholm, Suzanne Ardell, and Kirsti Nilsson. The November 1988 meeting could not have been so successful without the excellent support and facilities of the Pan American Health Organization and the Organization of American States. We also appreciate the support of the Guatemalan government with arrangements for the February 1989 meeting.

As the secretariat for the Commission, the Center for International Development Research (CIDR) at Duke University has provided first-rate support. We appreciate the interest and support of Duke President H. Keith H. Brodie and the Duke administration. William Ascher, co-director of CIDR and project director of the Commission, has contributed his intellect, discipline, and integrity to our work, and he has been ably supported by Mary Altomare, Ann Hubbard, and Charles Webster. We also express our gratitude to Sarah Anderson, Cathleen Mahon, Mike Regan, and other CIDR staff members who made things go so smoothly over the last months: Ginger Brent, Tom Campbell, Leej Copperfield, Suzanne Duryea, Brent Fogt, Steve Ganote, Jane Hunt, Susan Mees, Bevin Mitchell, Isabel Ovares, Joyce Persaud, Mary Jo Spencer, Martha Wall, and Terry Whalen. Their work was ably supplemented by Cecilia Truque of the Inter-American Institute of Human Rights.

Others have given unselfishly of their time, and we wish to thank them: Barbara Altman, Gustavo Arcia, Pedro Barria, Kirsten Baumgart, Margaret Buergenthal, Peggy Burkhardt, Stella Covre, Mariana Decker, Tito Drago, Joseph Eldridge, Jake Freiberger, Martin Gonzalez, Tomas Gronberg, Jacqueline Hartvelt, Vic Johnson, Ed King, Miguel Marti, Mary Mendell, Maria Otero, Rene Otero, Edgar Pape, Charles R. (Pete) Perry, Charles Roberts,

Charles Rooney, Andrew Rosen, Robert Rosen, Mike Skelly, Barry Sklar, Alain Thery, Jane Thery, and Lorna Watson.

Finally, we express our gratitude to U.S. Senator Terry Sanford, whose vision led to the formation of the Commission and whose statesmanship and support have inspired our work.

Preface

The work of the International Commission for Central American Recovery and Development gives hope—despite severe obstacles—for international and regional cooperation in support of peace, democracy, and development in Central America.

This Commission brings together 47 members from across the political spectrum and from 20 countries in Latin America, North America, Europe, and Asia. When we first came together in December 1987 the members of the Commission were new to each other and somewhat skeptical about the complexity of our undertaking.

Nevertheless, during initial meetings in San José, Costa Rica, we established a sense of trust and common goals and reached agreement on several fundamental points. First, the problems of the region require a regional approach. Only by working together can the five Central American republics resolve their social, political, and economic problems. Second, our efforts must support the Esquipulas peace agreement. We will encourage the kind of democratic development that addresses the poverty and inequality that lie at the root of the conflicts. In this effort, we would take the long view and not be discouraged by the inevitable setbacks on the difficult road to peace. Finally, we agreed that ours would be a plan proposed from the region, rather than imposed upon it. Central Americans would take the lead in every aspect of shaping the Commission's plan.

From this encouraging start, we began our work. We formed five working groups to address different aspects of development: immediate action, medium-term financial sustainability, long-term growth, regional cooperation, and democratic development and participation. These groups held a total of over twenty-five meetings and commissioned numerous detailed studies. The reports of these five groups were discussed at the second full Commission meeting, held in Stockholm, Sweden, in June 1988, and became the basis for the Commission's initial draft report.

From June until November the working groups focused on specific problems and refined their reports. At the same time an editorial committee of Commission members began to weave these reports into a single coherent document. This first draft of the final report was discussed vigorously and in depth during the Commission's third full meeting in Washington, D.C., in November 1988. Since that time, Commission members have made numerous changes in the report, producing this document which the Commission is pleased to present in Guatemala. Each commissioner strongly endorses the overall report, without necessarily agreeing with every interpretation or recommendation.

The process by which the 47 members of this Commission have come together and reached consensus should encourage other efforts to bridge differences and find common ground in a region divided. Rarely has any forum united such a diverse group. The Central American members of the Commission include businessmen, cooperative and union leaders, statesmen, bankers, and academics. Working together as a commission, they have come to understand and respect each other as never before. Despite their divergent backgrounds and perspectives, these Central Americans have reiterated their belief that "there is more that unites us than divides us."

Similarly, the international members of the Commission, including Latin American, North American, European, and Japanese leaders, all agree on the need for better coordination among developed and developing countries and international lenders and donors.

It is our hope that this very special spirit of cooperation and mutual understanding will guide future efforts for peace, democracy, and development in Central America.

In presenting this report, we feel that we have reached a starting point, not a finish line—that we have produced a realistic, compelling alternative for the Central American principals, as well as for the nations throughout the world who hope for peace in this troubled area.

The real work must now be undertaken by the governments, organizations, and individuals who have a stake in the peaceful development of Central America. Our document offers them concrete suggestions and policy options that form the basis for further discussions. The Commission, and its individual members, stand ready to advise or assist in any way we can.

Our efforts were aided by the research and writing of a host of scholars and experts—many from Central America. They provided invaluable background studies for the Commission and for its working groups.

Our colleagues on the Commission approached their work with courage, dedication, cooperation, and vision. Their industry, tenacity, and commitment to our undertaking symbolized the urgency of our undertaking. All of these qualities, however, could not have produced this remarkable result without the support and guidance of William Ascher, project director of the Commission. We owe a debt of gratitude to him and his talented staff at Duke University's Center for International Development Research.

Finally, we owe an enormous debt of gratitude to U.S. Senator Terry Sanford, who was instrumental in forming this Commission and who has been a statesman, coupling his utmost respect for the independence of the Commission with his commitment to provide whatever help we requested.

As co-chairs of the International Commission for Central American Recovery and Development, we express our gratitude for the opportunity to have been a part of this effort and this fine group of people. We hope that we have contributed in some measure as much as we have gained.

Through history and circumstance, diligence and courage, a rare moment of opportunity has arrived for Central America. The region is at a turning point. Our plan is offered not as a blueprint for a perfect world, but as a guidepost along the path to peace, democracy, and development in Central America.

Arthur Levitt, Jr.
Sonia Picado

Executive Summary

The International Commission for Central American Recovery and Development has carried out a comprehensive analysis of development prospects in Costa Rica, El Salvador, Guatemala, Honduras, and Nicaragua. The independent, nonpartisan Commission joins prominent economists, development experts, statesmen, social scientists, and business and labor leaders from across the political spectrum in Latin America, North America, Europe, and Japan to encourage the peace process, strengthen and stabilize democratic institutions, expand participation, and provide a solid base for economic and social development.

A decade of civil conflict and economic decline has devastated Central America. More than 160,000 people have died in wars or unrest. By 1990, ten million people—40 percent of the population—will be living in extreme poverty. The problems have deep roots in the endemic poverty and injustices that have long plagued the region.

Central America is caught in a vicious cycle in which war thwarts development and the lack of development fuels war. The Commission has reached strong consensus on steps that can help end that cycle. The fundamental premise is that lasting peace, genuine democracy, and equitable development are inextricable. These three objectives are mutually reinforcing. None is sufficient by itself; all are necessary. The Commission finds that:

−Refugees and displaced persons have been most severely hurt by the civil wars and are among the most vulnerable of the many millions of Central Americans living in extreme poverty. This is one of the most volatile political problems of the region.

−It will cost at least $2.55 billion over three years to assure the survival of Central America's neediest populations.

−The eradication of extreme poverty cannot be achieved through immediate actions alone, no matter how well-funded. It must also be the focus of medium- and long-term economic development.

−The persistence of civil and economic turmoil points to the need for new approaches to Central America's complex problems. Recent developments in and outside the region create new opportunities to implement the policies we advocate in this report. Central America has reached a turning point which calls for swift and decisive action.

Immediate Action

The Commission's immediate action plan is a catalyst for long-term, sustainable development rather than an emergency assistance package. The Commission recommends that an immediate action plan:

−Focus on refugees and displaced persons and those living in extreme poverty in the communities in which they are resettling or relocating.

−Make special provisions for children under age five, pregnant and nursing women, and the elderly.

−Generate productive employment by focusing on food security, health and nutrition, basic education, safe drinking water and sanitation, temporary housing, infrastructure, and human rights.

Sustained Development

The economic chaos in Central America cannot be alleviated without the cessation of armed conflict and the reestablishment of a favorable investment climate. But only through growth will Central America generate and sustain the resources needed to alleviate poverty and improve living standards for everyone. The Commission finds that:

−Investment and productivity have lagged badly, and policies are needed to develop untapped human potential and conserve the region's fragile natural resources.

−Improving the economic and social conditions of the region will require growth, increased employment, and improved distribution of the benefits of growth.

– The basic structure around which an effective development strategy can best be built are human resource development, more efficient production and export promotion, regional integration, and food security.

The Commission recommends a plan for sustained economic development that stresses the broader participation of women, workers, and indigenous populations. The Commission urges the five Central American countries to:

– Aggressively diversify and expand exports to earn foreign exchange and generate employment. A revitalized and restructured Central American Common Market can increase the region's capacity to export competitively.

– Reinstate a common tariff structure that gradually and deliberately reduces protection of domestic industry. The strategic importance of national food security and rural employment, however, justifies some protection for rice, corn, and beans.

– Reform tax systems and financial policies and revise agrarian policies.

– Reform the region's schools, placing highest priority on spending for primary education.

– Restore and reform Central America's health systems, particularly in rural areas.

Democracy

A primary cause of conflict in Central America is the lack of democracy. The Commission begins with the conviction that democracy reinforces equitable development and promotes peace. Democracy must include the participation of people who have previously been excluded, the peaceful resolution of conflict within and between nations, greater social and economic justice, respect for individual rights, and free and fair elections.

Despite the wars and other crises, there has been some progress in recent years toward democratic participation in Central America: more active political parties; large voter turnouts even when voters were at risk; and the re-emergence of labor unions and grass-roots groups.

The Commission recommends that democracy and popular participation in Central America be encouraged through:

–Continued withdrawal of the military from politics, and the development of effective mechanisms of civilian political control. Once hostilities abate, military budgets must be reduced so that funds can be channeled into education, infrastructure and other development projects.

–Immediate steps to assure the independence and security of judges and lawyers throughout the region.

–Creation of a Cultural and Educational Council to encourage democratic attitudes and human resources development.

–Establishment of the Economic and Social Council to contribute to democracy by serving as a regional consultative body of civil society.

Regional Cooperation

Revitalizing intra-regional trade is central to the region's recovery and development. Central American integration, however, should go beyond the revitalization of the Central American Common Market. This means strengthening and revamping the institutional structure, and building on existing institutions through the establishment of new organizations.

Regional institutions can help promote democracy. While war and economic crises have severely weakened the regional institutions created in the early 1960s, they can be revived and redirected to meet current challenges. The Commission recommends that the Central American governments work together to:

–Increase coordination of fiscal and monetary policies, as well as interest and exchange rates.

–Establish and advance the Central American Parliament to open channels for regional political dialogue.

–Create a Central American Court of Justice to help resolve conflicts and to find just solutions when they cannot be reached through other institutional mechanisms.

International Efforts

Long-term development will surely require at least a decade of sustained international support and encouragement. Central America is very sensitive to the actions of outside forces. The Commission finds that:

–For the next five years Central America will need $2 billion per year of
financial aid—up from current aid levels of $1.5 billion per year.

–To meet the immediate basic needs of targeted populations in extreme
poverty, at least $850 million will be needed each year for the next three
years.

The Commission recommends that the world community:

–Give its full support to the consolidation of peace and democracy as envisioned by the Esquipulas accords by withdrawing outside military aid to
irregular forces, and by basing its relations with Central American nations
on their compliance with Esquipulas.

–Encourage adherence to the Esquipulas accords through loans, financial
aid, and diplomatic initiatives.

–Not deny nations in compliance with Esquipulas financial assistance or
trade benefits on the basis of other political criteria.

–Help to finance the revival of the Common Market and the creation of other
regional institutions.

–Grant unilateral trade concessions, reduce tariffs, and increase quotas on
Central American exports for at least a decade.

–Lighten the debt burden: sharply reduce private debt, reschedule bilateral
official debt over a multiyear period, and expand financial flows into the
region from multilateral lending institutions.

–Encourage the United States to maintain current assistance levels and to
increase cooperation with multilateral aid efforts.

–Help establish a Central American Development Coordinating Commission
to foster coordination of aid policies and programs.

Introduction

In the 1980s, Central America has become synonymous with bloodshed, inequality, and poverty. Few economies on earth have gone so quickly from rapid growth to rapid decline, and the human and social costs have been enormous. Although the five countries have diverse histories, economic systems, and methods of governance, all have suffered.

Yet recent historic breakthroughs, both in Central America and in global affairs, create solid grounds for hope. To build on this progress in a spirit of realistic optimism, this Commission sets forth far-reaching, interrelated recommendations to foster peace, democracy, and economic development throughout Central America.

The Impact of the Crisis

A full decade of civil conflict and economic decline has caused tremendous human hardship in Central America. After nearly three decades of high but unevenly distributed economic growth, Central America since 1978 has gone backward by every measure of social well-being, including income, education, life expectancy, and health.

Violence has uprooted between 2 and 3 million Central Americans—up to 15 percent of the total population—from their homes and communities, leaving most without jobs, adequate income, or health services.

More than 160,000 Central Americans have died in wars or civil violence over the last decade.

In spite of massive external economic assistance, the living standards of the average person have actually declined by 25 percent. Not even peaceful and relatively prosperous Costa Rica has been able to escape the consequences of the crisis.

Today, three out of five Central Americans live in poverty, and two in five cannot afford their basic food needs. Three out of 10 Central Americans can neither read nor write.

Throughout the decade, governments of the region grew more distrustful of each other, and with external support built security forces far larger than the region had ever known. Compounding the problem, external powers have fueled tensions by emphasizing military solutions to economic and political problems. Continuing conflict within Central America poses the danger of further involvement of external powers.

Grounds for Hope

In the face of this deteriorating situation, Central Americans recently took decisive steps forward. In an impressive display of political cooperation that few in or outside the region expected, the five presidents met in May 1986 at the request of Guatemalan President Vinicio Cerezo to discuss ways of ending the wars and building peace.

After more than a year of intense discussions, the presidents signed the Esquipulas peace accords in August 1987. In recognition of this achievement, the Nobel committee conferred its Peace Prize upon the chief architect of the historic accords, Costa Rican President Oscar Arias.

The Esquipulas accords affirmed certain principles that are critical for the establishment of a secure region: the recognition of the legitimacy of each nation's government, a halt to the use of any nation's territory for hostile actions against another, and an end to external military support for irregular forces.[1]

Yet the Esquipulas accords went beyond relations among nations. They affirmed that permanent peace was impossible without democracy. The vision of Esquipulas calls for genuine, popular democratic processes and institutions in each country, and the resolution of domestic differences through dialogue, negotiation, and the ballot box.

Esquipulas has important economic implications as well. The five presidents foresaw not only an end to the bloodshed and the expansion and strengthening of democracy, but also the development of the region's human and economic potential.

In addition to regional progress, shifts in the relations between the super-powers have enhanced the possibilities of peace in the region. Central Americans are heartened by progress toward the peaceful settlement of regional conflicts in Afghanistan, Southeast Asia, southern Africa, and the Persian Gulf. Just as East-West rivalry has made such resolutions difficult in the past, cooperation among the superpowers can encourage peaceful settlements of Third World conflicts today.

The growing interest in Central America of the European Economic Community and the Nordic countries, Japan, Canada, and others further enhances the climate for progress toward peace.

Origins of the Commission

The Esquipulas accords properly focus first on the responsibilities and rights of Central Americans. At the same time, the accords explicitly call on the international community to assist the region in achieving the mutual objectives of political peace and economic development: "We have Central American avenues for peace and development, but we need help to make them effective. We ask for an international treatment that will ensure development so the peace we seek will be lasting. We firmly reiterate that peace and development are inseparable."

Inspired by this call to international action, United States Senator Terry Sanford proposed the formation of an international commission to put forth recommendations for regional reconstruction. The resulting International Commission for Central American Recovery and Development includes 47 members from across the political spectrum and from 20 nations in Central and South America, Europe, Asia, and North America. To guarantee its autonomy and integrity, the Commission is a nonpartisan, pluralistic entity independent of any government. Philanthropic foundations and development agencies fund the Commission's work. While maintaining its independence, the Commission cooperates closely with governments and private organizations throughout the world. It has working relationships with national, regional, and international organizations that work on issues ranging from trade and agriculture to education, finance, and human rights.

This Commission's purpose is to put forward a comprehensive strategy for economic, social, and political recovery and development in Central America. Its mission is to promote democratic development, and to end the paralyzing terror of violent social strife. The Commission seeks to strengthen the peace where it exists, spur efforts to end the fighting where it continues, and to encourage governments inside and outside the region to unite for peaceful, democratic development.

Peace, Democracy, and Development

The Commission's report is based on the fundamental premise that in Central America, durable peace, genuine democracy, and equitable development are indivisible. None is sufficient by itself; each is necessary for the attainment of the other. Without peace, there can be no development. But without equitable development, democracy cannot be sustained. And without democracy, there will be no lasting peace.

Further, the Commission believes that these three objectives are dynamically intertwined—that progress in one promotes progress in the others. The comprehensive development plan proposed by the Commission is intended to promote the peace process, heal the wounds of war, invest in reconstruction, enhance incentives for democracy, and build a strong regional and international framework for accomplishing these objectives.

Progress in Central America has too often been halted by debate over which steps should precede others. The Commission believes that all goals should be promoted together. Since the proposed development is designed to cement the future gains of the peace process, its initiation should not await peace, but should be pursued as an integral component of the struggle for peace.

The Commission seeks a Central America in which individuals feel secure in their own homes, families feel secure that their basic needs can be met, businesses feel secure from arbitrary interventions, and governments feel secure from internal or external violence. Such a secure Central America is the best guarantee of the legitimate security interests of external powers.

The Commission is fully aware of the obstacles that block the fulfillment of its objectives. While the Esquipulas accords created much hope and some concrete progress, many of its promises remain unfulfilled and the progress that has occurred is fragile. Nevertheless, the Commission believes that through history and circumstance, diligence and courage, a rare moment of international opportunity has arrived. It must be seized.

The Contents of the Report

The report is organized in six chapters—from the origins of the crisis through immediate needs and an economic development strategy, to strengthening internal democracy, regional integration, and international cooperation.

Chapter 1—The Recurring Causes of Crisis. The Commission has devoted much attention to the social and economic dimensions of Central America's crisis. It has done so not only because it believes that economic welfare is an essential component of human dignity, but also because it is convinced that a properly crafted strategy for economic reconstruction and development can help alleviate today's political tensions and can contribute significantly to the fundamental objectives of genuine democracy and sustainable peace. This is what the history of Central America—good and bad—demonstrates.

Chapter 2—Immediate Needs. Given limited financial resources and institutional capacities, the Commission chose to focus immediate efforts on the most destitute. At the same time, the Commission fully recognizes that this immediate action plan does not solve the region's poverty. Only a broad and sustainable development strategy can alleviate the poverty that oppresses many millions of other Central Americans. However, the guiding principles of the immediate action plan—its economic incentives and political organization—are fully consistent with the Commission's long-term development strategy.

The first priority of development in Central America must be the satisfaction of basic needs. Growth and equity are both indispensable. Only through the growth of the region's total wealth can the needs of the poor be met. But only concerted action can guarantee that the poor are given priority—so that the cycle of inequity leading to social unrest is not repeated.

Chapter 32—Sustained Development. The Commission proposes a strategy for sustained development that is based on four pillars: export promotion, regional integration, food security, and human resource development. To earn foreign exchange and generate employment, Central America should expand and diversify its export products and markets. Disincentives to trade should be removed, and governments should reduce distortions that prevent the efficient allocation of investment. Basic grains, however, are critical to the diets of the poor and warrant exceptional measures.

To foster both productivity and equity, the Commission calls for a concentrated effort to reform the region's educational systems and to increase spending on primary education. Efficiency and equality can also be enhanced by profound reforms of tax systems, the liberalization of financial policies, and the reduction of governmental inefficiency and overextension. Since over the long run development and poverty alleviation both depend on a sustainable resource base, it is also vital that Central America design an integrated environmental protection plan.

A strengthened Central American private sector can provide a powerful engine of growth. Governments must provide entrepreneurs a stable macroeconomic climate for investment and offer attractive rates of return. At the same time, the business sector should serve the public welfare by providing jobs through investment at home and by paying taxes as required by law.

Chapter 4—Political and Economic Democracy. The root cause of strife and poverty in Central America is the exclusion of much of the population from political life and the fruits of economic growth. Therefore, the Commission proposes a strategy of political and economic development that is inclusive and participatory.

Learning from the region's past political failures, the Commission has adopted an expansive definition of democracy. It affirms that democracy has several essential aspects: the participation of the entire population in institutions that represent their interests; the peaceful resolution of disputes through legal channels that facilitate dialogue, mediation, and peace; full observance of the rights of citizens; political succession by free elections; and social and economic justice. This report includes recommendations regarding specific institutions, laws, and processes to facilitate participatory democracy and to build attitudes of tolerance and mutual respect upon which democracy is based.

The Commission identifies the role of the armed forces as protecting the security of each Central American nation, and affirms the principle of civilian governance and the withdrawal of the military from politics. Moreover, once hostilities abate, military budgets should be reduced by decreasing the purchase of new arms and the number of military personnel. These funds should be channeled into education, infrastructure, and other development projects.

Chapter 5—Regional Integration. The revitalization of regional integration can contribute significantly to the strategic objectives of peace, democracy, and development.

The Central American Common Market should be revived and made compatible with an export-promotion strategy by progressively and deliberately reducing the external tariff. But a new integration scheme should go beyond trade to encompass macroeconomic policies. Central American nations should gradually increase the coordination of their fiscal and monetary policies, as well as interest-rate, exchange-rate, and capital-market policies. The integration of each Central American nation into the regional community would require conformity to the norms of democratic politics and efficient economics. Comprehensive interdependence would reduce regional tensions and contribute to regional peace.

Furthermore, the Commission believes that the new integration scheme should seek to involve a broad range of political and social organizations, including business, labor, and grass-roots movements. To further these objectives, the Commission endorses the creation of several multisectoral regional political institutions—a Central American Parliament, a Central American Economic and Social Council, a Central American Educational and Cultural Council, and a Central American Court of Justice.

Chapter 6—The International Contribution. The most urgent priority demanding the attention of the international community is the promotion of peace. Peace should be pursued directly, by helping to negotiate cease-fires and negotiations among warring parties, as well as by immediately beginning to implement reconstruction programs which reduce political tensions and create incentives for democratic practices.

The minimum cost of the three-year immediate action plan targeted toward refugees and displaced persons will total $2.5 billion. The Commission's macroeconomic projections of the region's total external financing needs suggest a net *annual* external financial inflow of $2 billion. Currently, net external financial inflows exceed $1.5 billion annually, so the Commission is recommending only a modest increase. This assumes that the region's debt is restructured in order to make debt service obligations consistent with the stipulated growth path.

The sources, channeling, and purposes of external assistance, however, should be fundamentally reorganized. The Commission calls upon the United States to maintain its current assistance levels, and urges that the required increase in assistance come from a diversity of sources, including the multilateral lending agencies and bilateral donors in Latin America, Europe, and Asia, particularly from the capital-surplus nations.

Foreign assistance should be channeled through mechanisms that ensure adequate coordination among donors and strong participation in decisionmaking by Central Americans. The Commission recommends the further development of the coordination mechanism established by the Central American vice presidents into a Central American Development Coordinating Commission (CADCC) for discussions among donor and recipient nations on aid policies and programs.

Much of the external assistance reaching Central America today is spent on security forces and on repairing war damage and keeping war-torn economies afloat. As conflicts subside and nations feel more secure, it will be possible to allocate a rising share of external resources for productive enterprises.

While the ultimate objective of the proposed development strategy is for Central America to become financially self-sustaining, it is vital that assistance funds and foreign commitment not dissipate prematurely; in the past, foreign assistance programs have dried up once perceived security threats disappeared.

Economic assistance is an instrument for peace. Donors should base their bilateral assistance on compliance with the Esquipulas accords, taking into account the advice of a collaborative, multilateral mechanism for assessing progress toward the goals of Esquipulas. It would be a violation of the peace process to exclude on political grounds nations that are judged to be in compliance with these goals. Furthermore, the Commission urges the international community to adhere to and support the economic policies outlined in this report. Donors should provide renewed impetus to countries making significant progress toward implementing this report's recommendations.

External capital can help launch Central America on a path of renewed growth, but growth will be sustained only if the region can earn foreign exchange through trade. Eventually, Central America should finance itself through export growth and nonconcessional credits and private investments. Therefore the Commission urges Central America's trading partners—the United States, Europe, Japan, and other Latin American nations—to sharply reduce their barriers to the region's exports and, where quotas determine trade flows, to grant preferential treatment to Central American products.

Learning from the Past

There have been several major development proposals for Central America over the years. The Commission has attempted to build on the experience of these previous efforts. The Alliance for Progress is memorable for its dedication to equitable development and social justice, even if much of its development strategy was more appropriate to that era than to today's more global economy.

The National Bipartisan Commission on Central America (the "Kissinger Commission") wisely advocated the elimination of trade barriers through the Caribbean Basin Initiative, while also correctly drawing attention to some of the linkages between democracy and development.

The Commission recognizes that previous efforts to tackle Central America's difficult political and economic problems have been undermined, in part, by the region's conflicts. Today, however, the time for concerted action is far more propitious. Within the region, economic reforms have begun in several nations, political structures and attitudes have shifted markedly, and elected leaders have themselves sketched a new vision for the attainment of peace and democracy.

More recently, in 1988 Central American governments worked with the United Nations Development Programme (UNDP) and the UN Economic Commission for Latin America and the Caribbean to develop a plan identifying specific development projects that would strengthen regional ties and provide production and employment in the recovery period. This "Plan of Economic Cooperation," overwhelmingly approved by the UN General Assembly, provides valuable lessons in its emphasis on Central America's own initiatives and priorities in the formulation of development plans.

This Commission is unique in that 20 of its 47 members are Central American. A Central American leads the Commission as its co-chair, and Central Americans have shared the leadership of its five working groups. Central American scholars and institutions also provided invaluable expertise. Rather than a plan imposed from outside the region, the Commission's recommendations are a product of the deliberations of an international body.

Chapter 1

Roots of the Crisis

Through these recommendations this Commission seeks to promote peace, democracy, and development by addressing the root problems of the current crisis. To put the Commission's strategy in proper context, three major factors in Central America's complex history must be understood: the failure of political institutions to mature during the period of economic expansion from 1950 to 1978; the inability of Central American economic structures to ensure sustainable, equitable development; and the added complications arising from the military involvement of governments outside Central America.

Exclusionary Politics

Throughout most of Central American history, political structures have not shown the ability to modernize and accommodate the interests of all members of society. In the 1970s, all Central American nations except Costa Rica lacked the key attributes of democracy: full participation, peaceful and tolerant means of conflict resolution, observance of civil and human rights, civilian governance through free elections, and social and economic justice.

Central American elites have often excluded other interests through economic, social, and political practices. The military frequently formed alliances with the traditional elite, enforced the closed political system, and assumed a crucial role in the management of governmental affairs. In some cases the military also prevented the development of political institutions and mechanisms that could have served not only to establish civilian control over the military itself, but also to allow less privileged groups to organize and to advance their interests.

As economic growth failed to translate into political and economic decisionmaking power for the majority, the political repression that predominated in most countries of the region sparked vigorous, widespread public frustration. Though economic expansion helped many poor Central Americans raise their standards of living, expanded the middle class, and improved social mobility, neither existing nor emerging social groups were permitted to participate democratically. Elections, when held, were frequently marred by fraud and the marginalization of many political groups. Through campaign restrictions, limited media access, threats, and violence, political parties were excluded from genuinely competing for power. Repression by authoritarian regimes in all countries of the region except Costa Rica eroded faith in political institutions and undermined the public legitimacy of national leaders.

Along with the absence of genuine democracy in Central America, government instability since World War II stymied peace and development. In Guatemala since 1950, chief executive power has changed hands three times through coups, twice through elections widely viewed as fraudulent, once through assassination, and once through U.S. intervention. In Nicaragua, the dictatorial Somoza family dominated politics for four decades. Even after the Sandinistas ousted Anastasio Somoza in 1979, following years of bloody civil war, an atmosphere of confrontation and intimidation still inhibits the achievement of democracy. Of the fifteen Salvadoran administrations since 1950, only two governments came to power through free, open elections. In Honduras, there have been five coups since 1950. Although in the 1980s efforts to overcome political instability and install lasting, democratic governments have made progress, gains toward true democracy remain fragile.

Historically, the active military involvement of foreign interests and powers in the affairs of the Central American states has too often exacerbated civil unrest and government instability in the region. This has occurred at various times since World War II. As local discontent grew, so did repression and political instability; as unrest grew into armed conflict, both governments and local insurgents found support from countries outside the region.

Although guerrilla groups had been active in the region for more than a decade, the late 1970s and early 1980s saw the greatest increase in armed conflict. Civil wars erupted in El Salvador and Nicaragua, and the widespread guerrilla insurgency intensified in Guatemala. Civilian opposition to counterinsurgency programs provided additional support to guerrilla groups.

From Growth to Crisis

Equally important to understanding the causes of the Central American crisis is that despite periods of strong economic growth, the gains from that growth were distributed extremely inequitably.

Central American economies expanded rapidly over the post-World War II period through export-led growth based on agro-industrial activities, accompanied by some import substitution. This growth was characterized by stable terms of trade and high investment rates. During this period of growth, Central America expanded trade with the international community and among the five nations themselves, and the region began to modernize and diversify its narrow economic base.

While aggregate measures of economic health improved, however, mechanisms for distributing the fruits of expansion to the majority of the population were absent or inadequate, and while many people struggled out of poverty over the course of these three decades, rapid population growth actually increased the numbers living in extreme poverty. Rapid urbanization and industrialization created new opportunities for the middle sectors, yet by the late 1970s job creation failed to keep pace with rapid growth in the work force because of labor-saving technologies and reduced business investment. This exacerbated the root causes of the crisis. At the end of the 1970s, growing social unrest alarmed local business communities throughout the region, resulting in a drastic reduction in private investment and substantial capital flight.

In the early 1980s, just as the violence was increasing, Central America's international terms of trade suffered the sharpest downturn in 40 years, as prices for Central America's four primary exports—bananas, sugar, coffee, and cotton—fell sharply and remained depressed throughout the decade. Faced with the resulting trade deficits and the burdens of growing external debts, the governments of the region began to face foreign exchange constraints and adopted diverse measures to ameliorate their respective imbalances. Efforts to curtail imports resulted in progressive restrictions on regional trade.

The Central American Common Market virtually collapsed after 1980, adding to the region's growing trade gap and depressing industrial activity while pushing Central American governments further into debt. The growing tensions among El Salvador, Guatemala, and Nicaragua during this period both reflected and reinforced the structural weaknesses of the Central American economies.

Economic Strengths

The unprecedented period of economic growth, averaging 6 percent annually from 1950 to 1978, demonstrated some strengths of the Central American economies. One was a competitive class of innovative entrepreneurs capable of adapting modern technologies and ideas to export production. Growth in exports came principally from three new areas of postwar expansion—cotton, sugar, and beef. During this period, the nominal value of Central American exports of goods and services to countries outside the region increased thirteen-fold, rising from $250 million to $3.2 billion.

The small size of domestic markets and the proximity to major export markets were other regional strengths which helped to create a willingness to adopt new forms of economic cooperation to take advantage of economies of scale. Just two years after six Western European countries organized the European Economic Community, the five Central American states in 1960 established the Central American Common Market (CACM), primarily to facilitate trade in nonagricultural goods. Industrialization followed a policy of import substitution and was stimulated in particular by the creation of the Central American Common Market and by protective tariffs.[2]

Exports expanded despite counterproductive policy measures, such as export taxes, overvalued exchange rates, and import tariffs. Further export expansion was often blocked by closed or restricted markets in North America and Western Europe, even as industrialized countries grew at a cumulative rate of 5 percent per year during the period following World War II and volume of world trade expanded at an annual rate of 9 percent.

Flawed Economic Structures

The economic growth that characterized the three decades up to 1978 rested heavily on the historic roots of the five Central American economies. Since their independence from Spain in 1821, the nations of Central America have had a history of uneven and unequal economic development. By centering their economies on a few agricultural exports—primarily bananas and coffee—they entered the world economy in the late 19th century vulnerable to international cycles of boom and recession. The benefits of growth had gone to a small elite and left out the mass of the population, including peasant farmers and indigenous peoples.

The Central American economies remain dependent on the production of a handful of agricultural goods for export. In the 1920s, coffee and bananas accounted for more than 70 percent of export earnings in all five republics, and more than 90 percent in Costa Rica, El Salvador, and Guatemala. Although the region diversified into cotton, cattle, and sugar in the 1960s, these five agricultural commodities still accounted for more than 70 percent of Central America's total exports, or more than one-third of the region's total gross domestic product in 1980.

Landlessness caused by the agricultural booms was an important factor contributing to social unrest or civil war. El Salvador's high population density and scarcity of land provided the most dramatic examples of the impact of the new commodity production. In 1971, an estimated 29 percent of Salvadoran peasants had no land, a figure which increased to 65 percent by 1980.

During the period of post-World War II expansion, there were modest improvements in the sharing of benefits in Guatemala and Honduras, with a serious deterioration in El Salvador and little change in Nicaragua and Costa Rica.[3]

Population Pressures. The region's population growth rate of 3 percent annually from 1950 to 1980 was one of the highest in Latin America. In just three decades, the population of Central America increased by two and a half times—from 9 to 22.5 million people. Because of this rapid population growth and the heavy concentration of the benefits of economic expansion, more people were living in poverty in 1980 than in the period immediately following the Second World War.[4]

The rapid population growth severely exacerbated competition for land —particularly in light of the large land requirements of cattle and cotton production—and for employment opportunities in overcrowded cities.[5] Unemployment for the region as a whole rose to 13.5 percent by 1986.[6] Underemployment has been estimated at nearly half the economically active population during the 1980s.[7]

Policy Failures. During the years of postwar growth, the Central American governments adopted policies that reinforced severe inefficiencies and inequities in their economic structures. Policy problems included protectionism, the neglect of agriculture, and inequitable credit systems. Fiscal policies adopted during this period were often overly complex, distorting, and ineffective. While in some cases governments failed to collect enough revenues to finance adequate programs to improve the human capital of the poorest social groups, after the oil crisis of 1973 they also undertook expensive subsidy schemes and overvalued exchange rates that reduced the prices of food, thereby hurting small-scale farmers. Although many developing economies have overcome such difficulties, Central America failed to enact necessary reforms and allowed policy errors to become deeply entrenched.

Decline of Intra-Regional Trade

The crisis of the 1980s has had a devastating impact on intra-regional trade. Instead of serving as a buffer against worsening external conditions, intra-regional trade has fallen drastically, from over $1 billion dollars in 1980 to less than $500 million in 1986. The adverse effect of this decline on the region's economies can be measured by the fall in exports—to both regional and international markets—from $4.9 billion in 1980 to $3.8 billion in 1987.

Numerous problems contributed to the decline in intra-regional trade. In the midst of severe balance of payments constraints and national political tensions, Central American governments devised increasingly divergent responses to the crisis. In place of fixed exchange rates, low inflation, and free intra-regional exchange, there are now multiple national protective systems, adopted primarily to cope with the adverse world economy. Other problems —including political disputes and the disparity of development among the countries—were also to blame for regional disunity. In addition, economic relations within the region changed dramatically following the Nicaraguan revolution, creating another challenge to economic reintegration.

External Economic Setbacks

While the violence and political upheavals of the late 1970s clearly disrupted growth, external factors further contributed to the economic decline. The drop in world prices for agricultural commodities, coupled with the oil shocks, reversed the terms of trade for Central America's non-oil-exporting economies.[8] The growth in world agricultural trade slowed to 1.3 percent in 1979–86, compared with 4 percent in the 1960s and 1970s. The prices of Latin America's 15 major export products dropped between 25 and 60 percent from 1981 to 1986. Central America's 1984 exports bought 30 percent less than they did five years earlier.

Of additional importance, especially for Costa Rica, was the sudden reduction in supply of commercial bank credit in the early 1980s. The dramatic rise of world interest rates, partly due to the U.S. deficit and efforts to limit inflation, significantly increased the burden of past debt. Debts increased, not to provide productive investment and support expansion of trade, but to meet past obligations. Costa Rica's external debt grew to 102 percent of gross domestic product in 1985. Nicaragua, because of dramatic reductions in exports, required large amounts of official financing. Its debt totaled $6.7 billion at the end of 1986, or more than three times its gross national product. Other countries were affected to lesser degrees.

War and severe economic recession induced by the world economic downturn have created a cascade of problems. The cumulative impact of the social and economic crisis has left Central America with between 1.8 and 2.8 million refugees and displaced persons. More than 160,000 war-related deaths and at least as many war casualties have left tens of thousands of families headed by widows.[9] Nature has also contributed to the human misery, inflicting severe earthquake, drought, and hurricane damage upon the region.

In addition to their costs in lives and human suffering, the wars have added heavy financial costs, including losses in the productive use of human capital. Instability and national insurgencies have led to huge increases in Central America's armed forces, diverting growing numbers of citizens from productive activities. Military personnel have increased for the region as a whole from about 48,000 in 1977 to more than 207,000 in 1985. Even in Costa Rica, there have been sharp increases in the civilian police force.

Indirectly, civil violence caused further damage by adding enormous defense budgets to the resource-strapped governments in the region and by scaring off investment capital. By 1984, approximately $2.5 billion owned by Central Americans was on deposit in U.S. banks. The total amount of Central American deposits held abroad was certainly much greater. Total spending on defense for the region as a whole, meanwhile, jumped from $140 million in 1977 to $600 million in 1986.

In terms of direct economic losses, El Salvador estimates that during the most intense period of the conflict, between 1979 and 1982, the country lost over $450 million in agricultural production and damage to infrastructure. It is estimated that damages and production losses from the Nicaraguan civil war have exceeded $700 million over the last seven years.

The Commission concludes that economic weakness, social injustice, political failure, and relentless violence are interrelated causes of the present crisis. Peace, democracy, and development can only progress together. The process must begin immediately, with support for the most pressing human needs.

Chapter 2

A Plan for Immediate Action

Central America's decade of crisis has most severely hurt the people least able to endure additional hardships—the poor. Over the last 10 years, the numbers of impoverished Central Americans have increased, and their living conditions have further deteriorated. Civil strife has uprooted millions of people from their homes, jobs, and means of subsistence. As the direct victims of the crisis, refugees and displaced persons are among the most vulnerable of the many millions of Central Americans living in extreme poverty.

The Commission firmly supports the five presidents' call for "urgent relief to the flows of refugees or displaced persons that the regional crisis has caused" as the most urgent challenge facing the region's postwar recovery and development.[10] Clearly, the issue of refugees and displaced persons is one of the most volatile political problems facing the Central American leaders.

This chapter proposes a comprehensive set of immediate actions in order to respond to the most pressing basic needs of Central Americans who face life-threatening conditions of poverty. These immediate actions, however, are designed to do more than feed the hungry. They offer pragmatic suggestions for reintegrating the displaced and refugee population, creating employment, establishing an infrastructure to ensure adequate food supplies, and setting up and maintaining health facilities for the poor.

The Commission also believes that the actions called for in this chapter will serve as a strong push to the consolidation of peace. If basic living conditions improve and the prospects for political participation are enhanced for the majority of the population living in abject poverty, guerrilla fighters and their supporters will be encouraged to see the possibility of prospering in a peaceful society with social and economic opportunities.

In assessing where the crisis has had the most severe impact, this report provides a framework for immediate needs assistance and estimates the magnitude of resources required to serve targeted groups. The Commission estimates that it will cost at least $2.55 billion over three years to resettle refugees and displaced persons. This will improve conditions for only a part of those now living in extreme poverty. Thus, the eradication of extreme poverty must be the primary focus not only of immediate actions, but also of medium- and long-term development.

The recommendations that follow are intended as a framework which the Central American countries can adapt in consultation with bilateral and multilateral development agencies.

The Social Impact of the Crisis

Ten years of global and regional crisis have multiplied the problems of the poorest people in Central America. The region is suffering from its most acute food supply shortage in decades. The world recession, structural adjustment policies, droughts and other environmental and natural disasters, increased unemployment, and armed conflicts have disrupted both the production and the distribution of food. With the rise in agro-export production, and consequently the declining production of basic grains, as much as 40 percent of the region's yearly food needs have been met with imported food.[11] Not surprisingly, prices of basic foods have risen.

The economic crisis and armed conflicts of the 1980s have also forced reductions in spending on health care and other essential social services. Large-scale migration to urban centers—an additional consequence of the wars—has sharply increased demands on social services. The numbers of trained medical personnel are inadequate, and governments lack the funding and administrative support necessary to implement effective national health programs.

As a result, barely half of all Central Americans now have access to basic health care. At the same time, key indices of health, such as nutrition and daily caloric intake, have declined. Particularly for the most vulnerable members of the population, including infants and young children of poor families, this combination has contributed to alarming declines in health. Throughout the region, over one child in every 10 dies before reaching the age of five. Of those children who survive, two-thirds suffer from some degree of malnutrition. In El Salvador, Guatemala, and Honduras, four of five children are malnourished or at risk of malnutrition.[12]

Other fundamentals of health and sanitation are equally inadequate. Some 10 million Central Americans do not have access to safe drinking water; in rural areas, these numbers represent 60 percent of the population. Drainage, trash disposal, and sewage systems are even scarcer.[13]

Education, which has never been broadly available except in Costa Rica, has also declined. Although elementary school enrollment and literacy rates improved significantly in the 1970s, there have been dramatic setbacks in the past 10 years. Many schools have been either closed or destroyed in the countries suffering from armed conflicts, and illiteracy now stands at 40 to 50 percent of the economically active population. For those who have been able to continue their studies, cuts in education budgets have contributed to a decline in quality. In fact, many displaced persons consider the lack of educational facilities and opportunities for their children in deciding whether or not to return.[14]

The physical destruction of communication and transportation systems in poor communities has hindered efforts at alleviating crisis conditions. Particularly in El Salvador, war has severely damaged the physical infrastructure. Rural war zones, where poverty is greatest, have been hardest hit, both by guerrilla and government military actions. War has destroyed roads, bridges, power plants, and electrical systems, and has forced the abandonment of schools, health clinics, and entire villages. Governments have not been able to reverse much of the wartime damage due to the constraints of the economic recession and the high priority given to defense spending.

Many of the Central Americans who return to their communities in wartorn regions will find that their houses have been destroyed or damaged by the violence. In El Salvador, about 40 percent of recent returnees found their homes completely destroyed, with the homes of another 25 percent requiring major repairs.[15]

The Imperative of Satisfying Basic Needs

Widespread poverty, the most serious affliction of Central America when the decade of crisis began, has gotten worse. In 1980, over 13 million Central Americans—or over 60 percent of the region's population—were below the poverty level, defined as the level of income insufficient to cover one's basic needs. Those living in "extreme poverty"—unable to cover the value of the minimum shopping basket of food considered necessary to meet their nutritional needs—totaled 8.5 million people.[16] By 1985, those numbers had risen even further, according to the United Nations, with 65 percent of the population living in poverty, and those living in extreme poverty totaling 10 million people.[17]

The huge number of those living in poverty and extreme poverty requires identifying the highest-priority groups within the impoverished populace. Refugees and displaced persons are designated as the highest-priority group because the conditions they face are the most severe. Targeting immediate assistance to one group, however, does not diminish the importance of addressing the needs of all impoverished people.

The goal of helping to meet the basic needs of those living in extreme poverty to break out of their circumstance is not simply a compelling humanitarian challenge; it is a fundamental element of long-term development. Moreover, in the long run it is feasible. This report focuses on the most vulnerable of all poor Central Americans and calculates the cost of their basic needs, with the realization that this larger goal—eliminating extreme poverty in Central America—can only be the fruit of long-term development policies which emphasize equity and the needs of the poor.

The Targeted Population

The Commission supports the Central American presidents in recognizing the plight of displaced persons and refugees as the number one challenge to recovery and development. This concern is shared by many institutions in the international community.[18] These uprooted persons have left their communities, homes, jobs, income, reliable sources of food, and (though these never existed for many) access to health care and other social services. Moreover, refugees and displaced persons often are denied the fundamental legal rights of other citizens. The extremely difficult conditions facing those who have fled homes and communities therefore not only imperil their lives, but also place in jeopardy efforts to attain social stability, national reconciliation, and longer-term development.

The Commission identifies four groups as the focus of an immediate action program. This targeted population totals 2,271,000 people. (See Appendix I.)

The first group is drawn from all persons who are either displaced within their countries, or are refugees in another country, and who are likely to return to their homes in Central America. Because the region's civil conflicts have taken place largely in rural areas, it is assumed that almost all displaced persons are of rural origin, and that returnees will go back to their original rural communities.[19] In addition, it is assumed that they have no resources for resettling, and that resettlement will mean an improvement in their living standards (even if they are still living in extreme poverty). A total of 618,000 Central Americans are in group 1.[20]

The second group consists of people living in extreme poverty in the rural communities receiving the displaced persons and refugees. It is assumed that this group, totaling 463,000 people, faces conditions of indigence similar to those confronting refugees and displaced persons.[21]

The third group includes the displaced persons who are already integrated —or may integrate—into communities other than their places of origin, and who are not likely to return to their home communities. They include both those internally displaced within their native countries and those who have left their native countries but remain within the borders of Central America. The Commission's cost estimates assume that most in this group left rural communities and resettled in urban centers. The total number of these refugees and displaced persons in Central America is 680,000.[22]

The fourth group includes those people who are living in extreme poverty in the urban communities where the displaced persons and refugees of group 3 have resettled. The estimates for the size of this group are based on the same data utilized for estimating the size of group 2.[23] This group totals 510,000 people. All four priority groups are summarized in Table 2 at the end of this chapter.

Women, Children, and the Elderly

Within the above population, a smaller group is identified that requires special care and specific programs—children under five years old, pregnant or nursing women, and elderly over 60 years of age. These "biologically vulnerable" people require special attention because they need significantly different treatment, are particularly susceptible to disease and illness, and cannot satisfy all of their basic needs by themselves. The total number of Central Americans who fit the above criteria for biological vulnerability is approximately 48 percent of the targeted population, or more than 1 million people.[24]

A Plan for Immediate Action

The immediate actions recommended in this report are not intended to be relief efforts like those that follow a natural disaster. Instead, this plan is intended to be the first step of a long-term effort to make structural changes that will enable Central Americans to benefit from the recovery and development of their region.

Actions prescribed here should be based on comprehensive, multisectoral programs. As the larger goals of the programs are not simply to provide assistance but also to enable the target population to assist themselves, programs should be limited in duration and should be tied to the organized participation and work of those who benefit.

Except for programs designed to assist the biologically vulnerable population, a critical factor of all programs should be employment and income generation. Employment-creation programs should revolve around the construction of infrastructure for the protection, renovation, and conservation of critical natural resources, the provision of social services, and the rebuilding of the physical infrastructure. Productive employment, even if it is short term, will help strengthen the basic skills of those who participate.

Though programs should be carefully coordinated and supported, they should also be decentralized in order to further promote participation, organization, and community self-sufficiency. Furthermore, efforts should be made to increase the management skills of persons living in the community and of those individuals and organizations working in immediate action programs. This training is necessary for the effective absorption of foreign aid and other resources devoted to such programs.[25] Hence, those participating in immediate actions should utilize the local resources, first-hand expertise, and international contacts of nongovernmental organizations. To facilitate the work of these nongovernmental organizations, governments should recognize their valuable contributions and provide the support their assistance requires.

Immediate Actions and Cost Estimates

The Commission recommends immediate actions to assist the target population in seven principal areas: food security, health and nutrition, basic education, safe drinking water and sanitation, temporary housing, infrastructure, and fundamental rights. These areas, together with job creation, are essential to meet basic needs, consistent with regional priorities as set forth by the Central American presidents and complementary to other efforts by the international community.[26]

The proposed immediate actions are based on careful cost estimates detailed in Appendix 1 of this report. The specific programs and their accompanying price tags, however, are intended to serve as a model that each country can elaborate and adapt in accordance with local conditions and development priorities.

For the minimum group targeted for immediate actions, total costs over a three-year period are $2.55 billion. As explained in Chapter 6, the Central American economies can effectively utilize only about $2 billion per year in total net external financial inflows over the next five years without creating serious economic distortions. Thus, although the costs of extending the full benefits of the immediate action plan to all Central Americans in extreme poverty would total $11.3 billion over three years, this level of aid is highly unrealistic in light of Central America's overall capacity to absorb resources effectively. Moreover, extending the direct food assistance program would jeopardize the promotion of domestic food production. In contrast, the Commission's target of $850 million per year is consistent with both Central America's absorptive capacity and the objective of promoting domestic food production.

The programs of immediate action include:

1. Food supply security

The key considerations in maintaining an adequate food supply are overall supply, local access, and price. Central America has both an absolute scarcity of basic foods and problems of access, particularly for displaced persons and for those who cannot afford the rising prices of the basic food basket. Immediate actions should focus on strengthening the production of food and improving access to basic foods by making them more affordable and by improving the infrastructure of food distribution.

Total costs of programs aimed at securing food supplies for the target population have been estimated at $1.5 billion. This figure includes food, logistical and technical support, and administrative costs. Although the costs of assuring food security represent nearly 60 percent of the entire immediate assistance effort, less than a third of the funds is devoted to providing food.

The major element is compensation for employment in community development, rebuilding the agricultural infrastructure, and improving food production. The essence of the strategy is to employ the targeted population as quickly and thoroughly as possible.

We recommend the following immediate actions:

(a) Direct provision of food to the target populations in rural and urban communities.[27]

(b) Provision of financial resources required to initiate production. Revolving funds and community banks should be made available for the production of basic grains and other food staples. Interest rates on the loans provided through these funds should reach market prices within three to five years.

(c) Food should be distributed in conjunction with work programs that generate income for participants. The income generated through the programs would serve to complement participating families' food requirements and other essential needs. These work programs should focus on community-based development projects.[28]

(d) Income-generating programs which accompany food programs should stress soil conservation and the protection of other natural resources, reforestation, and the construction of basic infrastructure for irrigation and water conservation.

(e) In urban communities, programs should be developed to create public food outlets and food cooperatives that could help guarantee adequate prices.

2. Health and Nutrition

Immediate actions should focus on a primary health care strategy, providing the target population with better access to all health services, controlling contagious diseases prevalent throughout the region, extending immunization and oral rehydration coverage, strengthening the management of health services, and improving the nutritional levels of those at greatest risk. Too little attention has been devoted to preventive health services.[29] Basic public health measures, such as providing safe drinking water to control intestinal disorders and to prevent the spread of other diseases, must be instituted.

The estimated cost for all of the above actions related to health and nutrition, including infrastructure, is $264 million. These monies are to complement and/or supplement ongoing initiatives at both regional and national levels.[30] Proposals for immediate action include:

(a) To increase the target population's access to health services, health posts should be constructed or rebuilt in rural communities, and clinics should be constructed in urban areas.[31] Labor for the construction and rehabilitation of these units would be provided by the income generating programs mentioned above.

(b) Medical supplies and services should be provided to the target population, with special attention to those who are biologically vulnerable.[32]

(c) Oral rehydration campaigns on ongoing programs should be carried out together with campaigns to eliminate intestinal parasites. Both campaigns should include treatment at health posts as well as efforts at public health education to minimize the risk of their recurrence.

(d) There should be special campaigns for the control of tropical diseases, particularly malaria, in rural areas.

(e) Current vaccination campaigns should continue and expand their coverage, paying particular attention to returnees under five years old and infants in resettled communities.

(f) Additional food should be provided to supplement pregnant and nursing mothers' daily intake, as well as for children under five years old.

(g) In both urban and rural settings, health units and posts should provide rehabilitation services for those maimed and wounded in armed conflicts. Psychological treatment should be provided for both communities and individuals.

(h) Public health and first-aid training should be provided to community workers, such as paramedic personnel, in order to carry out the above actions with a certain level of community autonomy.

3. Drinking Water and Waste Disposal

Programs in this area should strive to secure access to drinking water and basic sanitation measures for the target population. It is estimated that the immediate actions required to cover at least minimal conditions would cost approximately $178 million. Yet provisions should be made for medium- and long-range plans that will require substantial investment in infrastructure.

The following immediate actions are recommended:

(a) Emergency water supplies should be provided until safe drinking water services are reestablished or introduced in communities of the target population.[33]

(b) For urban centers, the numbers of community faucets should be increased so that there are no more than 50 families per faucet. Rural drinking water systems should be repaired or constructed.

(c) Programs to build latrines in the resettled communities should receive high priority. Where sewage systems already exist, these systems should be fully restored, connecting home latrines to main sanitary collectors. In urban centers, appropriate basic sanitation measures such as covering water waste disposal should be implemented. In both urban and rural settings, programs for proper garbage disposal should strive to improve municipal garbage collection services, incineration, and dump sites.

4. Temporary Housing

As refugees and displaced persons return to their places of origin, the first housing priority should be to provide building materials for temporary shelter for those whose homes were totally destroyed (an estimated 40 percent of returnees' homes have been destroyed). Simultaneously, building materials should be provided for repairing the homes damaged or partially destroyed (some 60 percent of homes require minor or substantial repair). Returnees should conduct these repairs themselves, when possible, but technical training and supervision should be provided to make better use of the materials. Technical assistance, building materials, and their transport to rural and urban communities is estimated at approximately $117 million.

5. Education

Immediate actions should focus on rebuilding formal educational services, including adult education and literacy programs, and should provide basic training in order to increase production and productivity. Total estimated costs on immediate actions revolving around education are $236 million.

The following actions are recommended:

(a) Schools should be repaired and constructed where needed. Labor for repair and construction should come from the income-generating programs mentioned above.

(b) More teachers should be hired to increase the number of teachers per student. Each school should be provided with at least the minimum equipment and materials necessary for instruction.

(c) Massive adult literacy programs should be carried out, insuring the participation of women.

(d) Literacy programs should be implemented along with technical training programs in order to increase agricultural production as well as to protect and conserve soil and water.

6. Fundamental rights

Immediate actions must be taken to protect basic individual rights of all citizens—but particularly for displaced persons and refugees. Guaranteeing these rights is essential to the target population's ability to participate actively in organized, effective ways to permanently satisfy their own basic needs. Programs should focus primarily on securing all legal documentation granted to other citizens in each country, and on supporting local efforts at organization.

The cost for these minimal actions is estimated at $48 million, but provisions should also be made to bolster and upgrade the juridical system. Respect for human rights, however, will require much more than capital investments. It will require the organization of the population to defend those rights, the political will of governments and armed forces, and the support of the international community. The Commission recommends:

(a) Those who have been displaced from their original communities should be provided with the necessary personal identity documents so that there is no distinction between them and the rest of the population.

(b) Population displacements have caused a great deal of difficulty over land titling and titles for other properties. Final and definitive titles should be provided to solve these problems.

(c) In urban communities, legal security of living quarters should be provided to those who live under permanent threat of being evicted from the land or buildings they occupy.

(d) Programs should be developed to organize and educate communities to enable the target population to participate actively in its own economic recovery. They should not be passive recipients of assistance, but rather active participants in the defense of their interests.

7. Physical Infrastructure

Immediate action should focus on repairing and rebuilding important municipal facilities and principal roadways to resettled communities. Immediate action should also be taken to provide emergency power supplies and to rebuild power and communications systems where they have been destroyed. In brief, the physical infrastructure must be in adequate condition to support sustainable food production and sound health; without programs to accomplish this goal, many key areas requiring immediate action would be placed in jeopardy.

We estimate that $217 million will be required to restore this basic infrastructure. The following actions are recommended:

(a) Markets, town halls, cemeteries, and other basic municipal facilities should be rebuilt or repaired. In urban communities, projects should be carried out to protect communities from rain damage, erosion, and landslides. Labor for these projects can be provided by the income-generating programs discussed above.

(b) Transportation access to resettled communities must be improved; it is essential not only to provide immediate assistance, but also to facilitate longer-term economic recovery.

(c) Emergency power sources should be provided to communities receiving returnees in order to ease and assist the process of resettlement.

(d) Where they existed, telephone and telegraph systems should be restored in order to improve communications between resettled communities and the rest of the country.

(e) Provisions should be made for medium- and long-term programs that would restore the social infrastructure. This should also hold for high schools, vocational schools and specialized health services.

Conclusions

Though this set of recommendations for immediate action represents a crucial step toward Central American recovery and development, it cannot solve the problem of Central American poverty. Solutions to the region's poverty go beyond the reaches of an aid package, no matter how great its magnitude; they must get to the roots of structures of development, and demand reform and a reordering of priorities. Long-term programs should seek to overcome the structural causes that underlie the conflict, to advance beyond the levels of coverage of basic services that existed before the crisis, increase access to land and permanent shelter, and broaden the opportunities for political participation.

Regardless of the quantity of funds obtained from external financial aid,[34] each government must also contribute to the administrative, logistical, and technical tasks. Foreign assistance programs can offer matching funds to encourage national governments to increase their immediate action commitments. Foreign aid not only can encourage the region's governments to make the satisfaction of basic needs the highest development priority, but can also help make such critical goals achievable.

Chapter 3

A Strategy for Sustained Development

The first priority in Central American development must be the satisfaction of the population's basic social and economic needs. While this is the most urgent priority, only through growth will Central America generate and sustain the additional resources needed to provide better benefits for the poor and, ultimately, to improve the living standards of all. But if this growth is not accompanied by greater political access and economic equity, then peace— and therefore sustained development—will not be possible.

The greatest challenge for Central America is to address the immediate needs of reconstruction and recovery and at the same time create the conditions for sustained development. Economic revival could get its impetus from the immediate action plan and the restoration of physical equipment and facilities that have been deteriorating over the past decade. These activities of reconstruction, combined with the revival of intra-regional trade and the assurance of adequate inflows of external capital, could lead to a phase of recovery that would take advantage of the idle industrial and agricultural capacity.

But consolidating long-term development requires more fundamental changes. It rests on basic changes in attitudes of all sectors of society: confidence, mutual trust, and a commitment to cooperation, efficiency, and equity. The Central American governments must reformulate their policies and promote changes in institutions to foster these attitudes so that recovery can be followed by sustained development.

A balanced development strategy must have three primary objectives: growth, increased employment, and improved distribution of the benefits of growth. These objectives can be achieved through three inter-linked sets of policies: stimulating productivity and investment, developing human resources, and reforming fiscal and monetary policies. In order to sustain development based on these policies, Central America's fragile ecology must be protected and its natural resources conserved and renovated.

The stimulation of productivity and investment must focus on domestic, regional, and international markets. Production and investment for the domestic market should include an emphasis on rapidly increasing the supply of basic foodstuffs for the Central American populations. In addition to taking advantage of the idle capacity in the industrial sector, reviving the regional market can be oriented to develop the competitiveness of Central American industry in the world markets. The recovery and expansion of diversified production for the international market is essential because the small Central American economies cannot grow on the strength of their domestic markets alone.

This multi-level revival involves removing the obstacles that impede exports to regional and international markets, while avoiding discrimination against production for domestic markets. The removal of barriers to trade, in fact, can contribute to domestic expansion.[35]

The second complementary set of policies is the development of the region's human resources. Building a healthy, educated work force will promote both growth and equity in the long run, although it requires some investment trade-offs. Investment in education and health, for example, may mean less investment in factories and farm equipment. In the long run, however, a strong human resource development strategy is a prerequisite for increased productivity; and in both the short and long run, it is a means of sharing benefits more widely.

Third, a prerequisite for successful export promotion and broader, more intensive human resource development is fiscal and monetary reform. Once Central America's domestic-oriented and export-oriented production has revived to the point where it generates sustainable surpluses, an evenhanded and economically neutral tax structure must be devised to channel a larger portion of the surplus into government spending on social services. Monetary and fiscal discipline is necessary to guarantee price stability and improved balance of payments that will restore and strengthen the climate for investment.

Promoting equity will also require specific and courageous efforts to mobilize and channel resources to the poorest, often excluded segments of the population. Agrarian policy must ensure more realistic agricultural prices and more productive access to land for the poor (especially where cultivable land is idle), which would also promote food security. Concerning the urban poor, the "informal sector" presents a strong but as yet untapped potential for increased production, employment, and equity through micro-enterprise development.

Economic Revival: Productivity and Production

The first key to economic revival is the cessation of armed conflict. An end to civil violence would help restore investor confidence and, if accompanied by guarantees against confiscation, would unleash some entrepreneurial activity. Dynamic private investment is essential for both recovery and sustained development. Assuming that the external financial flows outlined in this report are forthcoming, this economic activity could rapidly fill the domestic market vacuum created over the last 10 years. Nonetheless, sustained production for the domestic and regional markets requires improved allocation of resources to discourage uneconomical activities, and to increase productivity and efficiency of profitable enterprises.

Although export-oriented agricultural and industrial development has created the capacity for another export takeoff, the region's dependence on a narrow base of primary product exports exacerbated social and economic inequities and has left Central American economies vulnerable to sharp changes in international prices.

By diversifying its export products as well as its markets, Central America can reduce its vulnerability to price fluctuations and find new, dynamic growth opportunities. While traditional exports in both agricultural and manufactured products provide the greatest potential for short-term growth, Central America should also develop new manufactured and nontraditional agricultural exports to provide a cushion against drops in world prices.

International cooperation can contribute to this export effort by supporting infrastructure construction, short-term export financing, technology transfer, joint ventures, technical assistance, and marketing. International lenders and donors can also reward sound economic policy through the volume and terms of their loans and grants. But these contributions to the capacity to produce and export must be matched by actions to open up foreign markets for these exports. Preferential access to extra-regional markets is of great importance (see Chapter 6).

Currently, over half of Central America's exports go to the United States.

Central America should develop other markets, with special attention to its regional market. Reviving intra-regional trade—which has fallen from 28 percent to 7 percent of the five countries' trade—is an essential component of growth. Just to regain the volume of intra-regional trade reached in 1980 would fully utilize now-idle installed capacity and contribute to lower prices. As detailed in Chapter 5, the regional common market is also important as a platform for launching new industries to be competitive in international markets, but requires declining protection, progressive and deliberate reduction of discrimination against exports, and closer coordination of monetary and exchange rate policy among the countries of the region.

Reducing the discrimination against exports would not jeopardize the robust opportunities for domestic-oriented production. After a decade of war and the collapse of intra-regional trade, there is ample room for revitalizing production for the domestic and regional markets. Reduction of export discrimination would, however, better utilize scarce resources by steering investment out of highly inefficient domestic market production.

Assuring the Creation of Employment

In the wake of economic collapse and rapid population growth, roughly 45 percent of Central America's work force is now unemployed or underemployed. Employment creation should be a central concern in the minds of planners as they seek to stimulate production for domestic, regional, and international markets.

The expansion of employment must come from

1. economic recovery, insofar as it reemploys workers to operate already installed capacity;
2. an emphasis on labor-intensive production, particularly through micro-enterprise finance and in export-related production that takes advantage of Central America's abundant labor and relatively low wages;
3. the elimination of subsidized credit for large-scale enterprises that have been substituting artificially cheap capital for labor; and,
4. education, vocational training, and other human resource investments necessary to make the work force employable as production opportunities arise.

Developing Human Resources

The development strategy of economic revival and greater equity rests heavily on better-educated, better-trained, healthier Central American people. In a region where capital is scarce, labor is crucial to production. For Central America, labor constitutes a large, underutilized potential. The greatest long-term growth can be achieved through investing in this abundant but poorly developed resource.

Developing human resources will also help alleviate poverty and promote equity. In a region where three out of five citizens live in poverty, employment will help meet basic human needs and encourage social stability. This requires policies to raise the incomes of the poor, to improve basic education and health care, and to expand access to credit for male and female small farmers, self-employed laborers, and tradespeople.

Experience in other parts of the world affirms the value of investing in people. In both Japan and Western Europe, economies destroyed in World War II were transformed into "miracles" in less than 20 years with the help of sizable U.S. aid. The fastest-growing economies had put enormous resources into education, health services, and generation of employment for the displaced and the poor. Of course, Central America differs from Western Europe and the Far East in important ways, but these cases do demonstrate that there is no necessary long-term trade-off between growth and human resource development. A prime example of human resource development has clearly been Japan, where investments in education and health have been tailored to Japan's outward-looking development strategy.

A Focus on Education. Education is a fundamental element of human resource development. Education not only increases productivity and incomes, but also encourages social mobility and integration, and helps to impart values of justice, democracy, and respect for human rights.

Throughout Central America, the quality and accessibility of education are deficient. Although primary school enrollment and literacy improved in the 1970s, these educational advances have suffered reversals during the crisis of the 1980s. Today, three in 10 Salvadoran children do not attend elementary school. Many elementary school teachers have only a high school education. And in the coming years, population growth will put additional strains on the region's already burdened educational systems. With more than 30 percent of the region's population under 10 years old, 4.7 million children will reach school age between 1996 and the year 2000.

The Commission recommends increased investment in education, particularly in literacy and primary education. This must include greater expenditures for improving instructional materials and facilities as well as for better training for primary school instructors. Because the economic returns from investment in primary education are remarkably high, educational investment is extremely effective in promoting productivity and efficiency. Averaging 26 percent throughout Latin America, returns are highest for investments in teachers, other personnel, and general curricula.[36]

Without doubt, every level of education in Central America could benefit from increased funding. With limited resources, however, literacy and primary education should receive higher priority than secondary and higher education. Basic education provides the greatest and broadest benefits at the lowest cost; it gives people the basic tools to participate in society; and it provides the foundation on which all advanced educational achievements must be built.

Even without increased funding in the near future, secondary and higher education can be restructured to be made more relevant. Secondary education should have a stronger technical and vocational orientation. Regarding higher education, governments should reconsider "open admissions" policies that overburden university facilities by admitting unqualified students with little prospect to graduate or to use their educations productively. Given scarce resources, Central American universities should also institute regional programs for specialized curricula.

The private sector can play an important role in improving the quality and relevance of education and may be able to fill the gap of limited public funds available for secondary and higher education. Key steps to raise technological expertise, increase productivity, and improve private and public management include cooperation between educational institutions and business (through company-sponsored training programs and school construction), volunteer teaching by well-educated private-sector employees, and privately financed scholarships.

The private sector, regional governments, and the international community should cooperate to provide loans and scholarships for Central American students. The opening of a Regional Student Bank, for example, could be organized within the structure of the Central American Bank for Economic Integration. The international community can contribute to the development of managerial and technical expertise through training and education on the broadest regional basis.[37] The Commission also recommends that the international community support technical and professional training programs both inside Central America and in their own countries.

Health Care and Family Planning. Adequate health care is also critical for the success of human resources development in affecting performance in the workplace, the classroom, and relations with the rest of society. Yet half of all Central Americans lack access to basic health care, safe drinking water, and sewage or waste disposal services. The immediate action plan, discussed in Chapter 2, addresses these needs for the region's most vulnerable populations. Extending basic health, sanitation, and nutritional services to the entire population should be a priority for the Central American governments and for international donors.

Annual health ministry budgets average under 3 percent of national budgets, and health expenditures are less than $10 per person in several countries. Compared to an average of 40 to 80 times that amount in developed countries, these spending levels are dangerously low.[38]

Not only is greater spending on health care necessary, but a fundamental transformation of national health systems is also required. Scarce resources are still concentrated in the major urban centers, in hospitals rather than health clinics, and in curative rather than preventive services. Local health services should be the core of a transformed system, offering every citizen access to basic services and providing the entry point to more complex secondary and tertiary levels of care. The bulk of new resources must be targeted at community-based health centers with greater capacities to serve marginal groups and to promote prevention and control of infectious diseases.

In order to reform national health systems, three basic changes in the health infrastructure and policies must be made:

– First, the lack of coordination between health ministries and the social security institutions must be remedied to ensure the most efficient use of scarce resources.
– Second, the supply and training of health personnel, including community health workers, technicians, nurses, sanitation specialists, and doctors, should be increased to improve the extremely low ratios of health workers to population.[39]

– Third, region-wide primary health care strategies should be implemented through the decentralization and strengthening of local health services and community participation.

The first priority of this revised national health system ought to be to lower maternal and infant mortality rates and to improve the health of mothers and children. Induced abortions probably account for the highest proportion of maternal deaths in all five Central American countries, and are the most frequent cause of hospital admissions among women. Infant and maternal mortality rates are also rising throughout the region due to cutbacks in health services and to malnutrition and anemia caused by increasing poverty. Many deaths are easily preventable with inexpensive and available measures. Improved nutrition would reduce maternal and infant mortality, especially if accompanied by immunization, oral rehydration, and treatment of acute respiratory infections. Without these improvements, high infant mortality leads to higher birthrates, since birthrates tend to be highest where the child's prospect for survival is lowest.

Central America has the highest birthrates in Latin America.[40] Children and mothers are endangered by closely spaced births that result in premature deliveries and weak and underdeveloped infants. Societies suffer as overpopulation puts pressures on land, labor markets, government services, and the environment. The Commission strongly recommends developing sex education programs for adolescents and adults and expanding reproductive health care that includes family planning. Priority should be given to rural areas, where birthrates and maternal death rates are highest.

Including the Previously Excluded. The human resource development strategy must seek to make all citizens productive participants in the democratic development of the region. For those who have traditionally been excluded from development, extra efforts must be made to bring them into the economic mainstream. In the context of the Commission's development strategy, this means extending to these people access to education, training, credit, health care, and family planning. Women, indigenous groups, and workers are illustrative of social groups that have been ignored or excluded. Special efforts must be made to include them in the process of Central American growth and development.

Women are currently denied access to the resources and opportunities they need to participate fully in society. Women grow 30 to 40 percent of the food crops, but their rights to own land are restricted for both legal and cultural reasons. Women are also denied credit and technical assistance from agricultural extension services for their productive activities. Women who work as agricultural day laborers are paid less than men.

Illiteracy rates for women are higher than those for men, as are school dropout rates. Since women are more likely to be undereducated and underemployed, even modest education yields significant returns, both to the women and to their societies. In fact, investment in women's education yields returns nearly a third higher than investment in men's education.[41]

Women also constitute a majority of the so-called informal sector—the vendors, artisans, and other small-scale entrepreneurs who operate without legal protection and benefits and whose income goes unreported. Sixty-five percent of the smallest concerns are owned and managed by women. For many, lack of education and family responsibilities prevent their entry into formal-sector professions.[42]

The Commission recommends that women receive equal access to credit, land, education, and extension services. Laws that discriminate against women should be revised, and laws that provide equity should be enforced. Improving women's access to resources and opportunities, however, requires specific targeting of women as the beneficiaries, since there is ample evidence that male heads of households often do not share benefits with women and children. During the period of reconstruction, priority access to services and productive resources should be given to widows with small children and female heads of households who have been displaced by the wars. Women's organizations should be actively involved in planning and implementing these programs.

Native Americans are among the poorest of the poor in Central America and have consistently been denied access to economic resources and political participation. They represent another untapped human resource. To develop their productive potential, indigenous peoples must be supported in pursuit of their own definitions of economic prosperity and cultural autonomy. The Commission recommends that governments recognize the political and legal rights of indigenous populations, as both citizens and members of distinct ethnic groups, and their cultural and religious diversity.

The best response to the social and economic problems that affect each country can only be formulated through consultation among government, management, and labor. When workers participate in economic decisionmaking, they have a greater stake in the success of an enterprise. Wages through-out the region are low enough to be competitive in the international market, and wage increases that are geared to productivity increases would not jeopardize this competitiveness. Labor-intensive techniques and strategies are important for employment generation, especially in the near future.

Workers and their representatives must have the opportunity to express their concerns about wages and working conditions. The Commission recommends the creation of opportunities for workers' participation in ownership and profits. Central American governments must assure the safety of labor leaders and members and should enforce International Labor Organization codes.

The Potential of Micro-Enterprises. Assisting very small businesses, or "micro-enterprises," is another very effective action the Central American governments can take to develop human resources. Micro-enterprises—defined by the World Bank as firms with fewer than 10 workers and less than $10,000 capital—already represent a large share of the region's economies. Some 48 percent of the employed population now works in micro-enterprises. In El Salvador, micro-enterprises represent 94 percent of all enterprises, or 39 percent of the nonagricultural jobs; in Honduras, 95 percent of enterprises are micro-enterprises.

Making small amounts of credit available to male and female farmers, fishermen, artisans, self-employed workers, and tradespeople is an efficient means to promote both productivity and equity; a relatively small amount of credit can generate a very large return. The Inter-American Development Bank reports that the average cost of generating a job and a business is $1,000, and the average loan by nonprofit lenders is $682. These small loans produce dramatic income growth and have surprisingly high repayment rates.[43]

The absorptive capacity of micro-enterprises is impressive. Estimates of the resources that micro-entrepreneurs throughout the region could quickly and productively use range from $180 million to $250 million. Yet in spite of exemplary repayment rates, banks are reluctant to make such small loans, in part because of higher administrative costs. Most micro-enterprises borrow from informal sources, sometimes paying 10 times the bank rate of interest. In Costa Rica, fewer than 1 percent of commercial bank loans go to micro-enterprises.

The Commission recommends earmarking more credit for micro-enterprises.[44] These loans could be handled more efficiently and effectively by local development organizations, credit unions, or cooperatives. Foreign assistance agencies and central or commercial banks could lend larger sums to these organizations, which are often better equipped to process small loans.

However, for credit to micro-enterprise to be effective, it must be accompanied by a package of technical assistance in manufacturing, marketing, and administration. Government and the international community should also support cooperative arrangements among micro-enterprises to purchase inputs, establish creditworthiness, share equipment, and market their products. Finally, governments are urged to reduce the costs and complexity of official transactions that micro-enterprises must undertake.

Agrarian Policy and Food Security. Agricultural production is of fundamental importance in the region. Modernization and diversification of agricultural production are basic elements of the Commission's economic strategy. The agrarian situation is a very serious problem in Central America; the poor conditions of agrarian workers have contributed to the instability of the past 10 years. It is imperative to improve the living conditions of agricultural workers and help them become landowners. In doing so, it is necessary to strive for peace among the groups involved and to preserve productivity and efficiency while promoting equity.

In light of the diverse agrarian conditions in Central America, different approaches ought to be taken. Where land is abundant, idle land should be purchased with due compensation to its owners and distributed to create new farming enterprises. Where land is scarce, greater investments and reorientation of land use (for example, through expanded irrigation to increase the number of growing seasons) is essential for increasing the availability of steady employment.

Peasant farming is a very important component of the agricultural sector. Central American governments should assist small farmers with credit and technical advice so that they can become viable businesses and should work to provide alternative nonfarm employment to landless peasants. Rural nonfarm employment, especially in agriculture-related industries, provides the key to rural employment and to integrating rural and urban development.

The strategic importance of national food security and of rural employment justifies special measures. The Commission recognizes the need to protect and promote the production of three essential food crops—rice, corn, and beans. Food production should also be promoted through the elimination of overvalued exchange rates and through a package of credit, technical assistance, and infrastructure support for small farmers. Direct assistance to small farmers represents well-targeted financial support.[45]

Fiscal and Monetary Reform

The distortions in Central American monetary, credit, and fiscal systems are serious obstacles to advancing beyond short-term economic recovery. The same policy reforms required to revitalize production for the domestic and regional markets are essential for unleashing Central America's export potential.

The Commission strongly recommends a stable and realistic exchange rate policy. The aim is a unified rate corresponding to market conditions. This is as important for achieving the monetary compatibility needed for regional integration as it is for removing the obvious disincentive that overvalued exchange rates pose for exports in general.

The Commission also strongly urges a common tariff structure that progressively reduces protection of domestic industry. Commercial policy should aim for modest levels of protection of no more than 30 percent in five to seven years via regular and predictable reductions. There should be only limited variation in effective protection across sectors. Here, too, regional integration will be best served by nonprotectionist policies that will avoid recurrence of intra-regional debts (discussed at length in Chapter 5). By the same token, the revival of regional integration can contribute to the pressure to eliminate domestic protectionism that arose to serve special interests or to meet past emergencies.

These two central pillars of trade policy—stable exchange rates and a common tariff structure—should serve as an integral part of the medium-term transition while adequate external resources are assured. Tariff rationalization must be accompanied by availability of credit for modernization and investment by domestic firms. With more stable and predictable capital inflows (see Chapter 6), central banks could use reserves to reduce speculation and gain credibility for the new policies.

Successful trade policy also depends on adequate infrastructure (including roads, ports, airports, communications, and transport facilities); adequate finance and insurance systems; trading companies; technical assistance; and human resource development at all levels of export-production skills, including improvements in business and managerial skills.

Investment and the Financial System. Medium- and long-term development in Central America requires significantly higher levels of domestic savings and investment. Foreign investment and other external financial flows ought to be welcome and encouraged, but even a generous external effort cannot substitute for higher domestic investment. To provide the infrastructure to support the rise in saving and investment, national financial systems require extensive reform. Within a framework of gradual structural adjustment, financial liberalization—the reduction of regulations and limits on financial transactions—can make a positive contribution. Clearly, a central objective must be moderately positive real rates of return on domestic deposits in the financial system. Although improved political conditions could remove one impediment to the return of capital, realistic domestic returns are also necessary. This can be attained only if central bank regulation focuses on consistent implementation of monetary and credit policy and effective bank supervision, rather than regulating interest rate limits and providing liquidity to problem institutions through rediscounts.

But financial liberalization must be conceived in the context of a broad array of supporting policies, including significant reduction of fiscal deficits and improvement in the trade accounts, as well as an effective supervisory framework. A next stage should see the development of a broader market for public securities to provide more credit to the private sector and a broader range of assets for savers.

Growth with Equity: The Importance of Tax Reform. As export growth and domestic market revival produce increased income, these earnings must finance human resource investment. More predictable, broader-based, and more equitable taxes are essential for financing vital public functions such as education, health, and physical infrastructure investment. To sustain progress toward economic and political democracy, tax revenues must increase, and tax administration and collection must be improved.

With their dependence upon primary exports, Central American countries have relied heavily on export taxes. Given the fluctuations in international prices, these capture some of the windfall gains of suddenly-improved commodity prices. But for that very reason, their collection is unstable.

Due to exemptions and special incentives that complicate administration and divert revenues, direct taxes such as income and property taxes have suffered from declining yields. The impact of indirect taxes, such as sales and import taxes, has been weakened by long lists of exemptions. Discriminatory taxes on foreign enterprises either discourage investment or lead to arrangements that deprive governments of legitimate revenues.

The Commission recommends increasing the importance of a single-rate value-added tax within each country to improve the soundness and equity of the tax systems, which suffer from large-scale avoidance and evasion of direct taxes. The value-added tax would also avoid distortions in relative prices resulting from different tax rules, substitute for many specific excise taxes, and ease administration. Furthermore, a value-added tax would facilitate international and intra-regional trade by allowing the full indirect tax content in exports to be removed at the time of export.

Insofar as direct taxes remain a part of Central American tax systems, the Commission recommends simplification and the elimination of special treatments. World experience has shown that extremely high marginal rates do not yield high revenues, especially where tax administration is weak.[46] A far better approach is to broaden the tax base, provide greater horizontal equity across sectors (rather than taxing export and domestic-oriented enterprises differently), and eliminate exemptions designed to steer investment. These steps would increase the effectiveness of the tax system while reducing the distorting impact of differential treatments.

The timing of tax reform is crucial. There can be a lag of several years before reforms are implemented, with implementation tied to resumption of growth, but the planning should begin right away. Planning a fundamental tax reform must be based on consultations with all groups, and must recognize that simplicity is essential to ease administration and to eliminate the abuse of loopholes.

Fiscal management requires discipline on the part of the Central American governments. Since successful exporting appears to generate "easy surpluses," there is always a temptation to intervene directly into the exporting transaction to extract gains through overvalued exchange rates that redeem hard currency with less local currency, or through export taxes and "windfall profits" taxes. Export earnings should be taxed, but only as other earnings are taxed, so as not to depress artificially the "after-tax returns" on export activities. If export is profitable, then effectively administered uniform direct or indirect taxes on individual incomes or consumption will yield revenues without discouraging export activities or inducing exporters to evade taxation. This is especially important as exporters are in an excellent position to remove their capital from the economy.

More Effective Government. The increased competitiveness necessary for this development strategy depends in part on actions by the public sector, which needs to be strengthened and modernized in those areas in which government intervention must be made more effective. Although reductions in regional conflicts offer the promise of smaller defense budgets, governments cannot count on rapid declines in military expenditures to solve the fiscal deficit problems. Clearly, large fiscal deficits must be brought under control by tightening public spending, reforming inefficient government programs, and reducing bureaucratic inefficiency. While the provision of social services could be better managed and more carefully targeted, overall services are already tragically low and should not be cut further.

State enterprises are candidates for close scrutiny. Compared to other Latin American countries, state enterprises in Central America are few in number, but their role is important enough for their efficiency to be of concern. Governments should choose between public and private operations on the basis of economic efficiency and sound economics, examining each state enterprise on a case-by-case basis rather than through an ideological predisposition either to maintain public management or to privatize.

The seemingly poor performance of state enterprises is often due to policies beyond their control—such as maintaining unrealistically low output prices, extending high subsidies, or burdening state enterprises with excessive debt. Therefore, reforming the policy environment for public enterprises is equally important. As much as possible, public sector enterprises ought to face the same competitive, market-regulated conditions as the private sector. They should not enjoy special privileges on input prices, tax treatment, tariff protection, and access to credit; neither should they be subject to the burdens of price controls and indebtedness. Public enterprises should operate within a decentralized government structure and should not be linked to central government budgets.

Conserving Natural Resources

Sustainable development, especially if one of its major components is the export of agricultural products, requires much more care of Central America's natural resource endowment than it has been receiving. Deforestation and soil erosion have become serious threats to resource-based sustainable development and therefore must be addressed by government policy as part of the economic strategy.

With the partial exception of Costa Rica, responsible natural resource use has been badly neglected:

- half of Central America's farms use land very inefficiently
- the vast majority of pasture land is completely unmanaged
- fragile marginal lands are being added rapidly into production despite underutilization of better lands
- pesticides are often abused
- soil erosion is undermining hydroelectric dams, port facilities, and river ecosystems
- overfishing has depleted near-shore species while potentially lucrative off-shore fishing has been neglected.[47]

Strengthening and enforcing environmental regulation must be combined with resolve on the part of Central American governments to withhold support or approval for ventures that are productive only at the cost of depleting the resource base and damaging the environment. While Central American entrepreneurs should not be discouraged from pursuing the region's comparative advantages in exports, the costs of depleting or damaging the natural resource endowment must be taken into account.

The Commission recommends that governments use extreme caution regarding colonization programs that promote farming on environmentally fragile land. While such programs have permitted modest increases in production, they have had negative effects on forests and rivers. They also have contributed to the spread of malaria and other infectious diseases, because the public health consequences of large-scale colonization are rarely taken into account. Moreover, the newly acquired land has been frequently consolidated into large farms, further contributing to land concentration. In light of the potential for increasing agricultural productivity on existing farmland through better policy and more intensive management, further colonization into lands of uncertain long-term productivity is ill-advised.

Similarly, the misuse of pesticides and fertilizers, even if motivated to produce greater agricultural yields, should be regulated more carefully by Central American governments. Technical assistance for monitoring chemical pollution would be an important contribution to this end.

The Commission underscores the importance of poverty alleviation as an instrument of environmental protection. Employment that alleviates the necessity for poor people to establish small farms on hilltops, forest land, or other marginal areas contributes directly to conservation.

There must be greater recognition of the *regional* nature of Central America's environmental problems. These include watershed management, the conservation of shared river basins, regional energy systems (such as electricity grids), and preservation of coastal areas.

Therefore the Commission recommends an integrated, regional environmental plan to address these and other environmental concerns. The Commission suggests that the Central American Parliament establish a multisectoral body to develop this plan and to undertake periodic environmental impact analyses. Without a comprehensive plan that seeks to promote the rational use of land, water, and renewable and nonrenewable resources, the costs of acceding to requests for bending the environmental rules are difficult to judge, and the discipline of complying with a multilateral agreement would be lacking. An integrated plan should be devised through the cooperation of governments, nongovernmental organizations, universities, research centers and the private sector. This same multisectoral structure should be involved in implementation.

Part of the technical preparation of a regional environmental plan must be a far more intensive inventory of Central America's natural resource endowment. More knowledge of the region's water, land, flora, and fauna will facilitate the estimation of the environmental costs of specific projects. It would also permit an "environmental accounting" system that could indicate when apparent economic advances are coming at the expense of environmental and resource losses that jeopardize future development.

The protection of fragile ecosystems is difficult during a period of economic crisis. The international community can help by engaging in "debt for environment swaps" through which foreign debt is redeemed in local currency to purchase virgin lands of low agricultural potential. In the long run, Central America will face the need to renovate the areas that have suffered from environmental damage during this period of crisis.

Sequencing the Components of the Development Strategy

The appropriation of hard-earned profits from export growth and domestic recovery to finance human resource development must be gradual and deliberate, with great care taken to avoid leaving the economies starved for capital or vulnerable to renewed capital flight. Fiscal policy reform is essential, but it must be formulated in recognition of the fact that positive real returns are necessary for investment. Redistribution in times of depression or even fragile recovery is neither politically nor economically feasible. In the meantime, tighter targeting of governmental human resource investments toward the poor and greater efficiency in providing human resource services will have to suffice as far as the domestic effort is concerned until a more robust Central American economy begins to generate significant surpluses. Thus external assistance takes on a crucial role in nourishing a human resources strategy until the domestic effort can get under way on a sustainable basis.

Chapter 4

Building Democracy

The difficult history of democratic governments in Central America demonstrates again that peace, democracy, and development are inseparable in this region. As Chapter 2 points out, despite the strong economic growth from 1950 to 1978, a lack of democracy combined with inequality and highly mobilized opposition contributed greatly to the civil wars of the past 10 years in El Salvador, Guatemala, and Nicaragua. Similarly, as economic stagnation of the past decade has followed in the wake of physical destruction, the collapse of regional trade, and massive capital flight, it has become clear that peace is a prerequisite for long-term development.

It is also a basic belief of the Commission that democracy reinforces equitable development and promotes peace. The model of Costa Rican democracy, uninterrupted since 1948, shows that political pressures can induce governments to assist lower-income groups, thus improving human resources to promote development. The Costa Rican example also demonstrates that democratic practices can be preserved in an economy oriented to export-driven growth, and that democracy and equity do not have to undercut economic responsiveness to new productive opportunities.[48]

Despite the wars and economic crises, some progress in the mechanisms that encourage democratic participation has taken place in the last few years. Numerous political parties have become active. More credible and legitimate electoral processes have emerged, supported by large voter turnouts even when voting entails personal risk. There have been some changes in economic structure, such as increased benefits for workers and reforms in land titling and ownership. Labor unions and pressure groups have reemerged, and the number of grass-roots groups and local development organizations has increased tremendously.

Although fragile, these developments are a start. In order for democracy to sustain peace as well as equitable development, the governments and citizens of Central America must make strong and sustained progress toward incorporating the essential and mutually dependent elements of democracy into their societies. These elements are:

- the participation of the previously excluded in institutions that represent their interests;
- tolerance of conflicting views;
- the peaceful resolution of internal and external conflict;
- civilian rule and respect for civilian institutions and constitutional guidelines;
- fair and impartial justice from an independent judiciary;
- social and economic justice;
- full observance of the rights and freedoms of citizens;
- political competition and succession of government through free elections, with the peaceful passage of power by one administration to another it may not trust.

Broadening Participation

An essential element of the democratic vision of Esquipulas is the broadening of participation. Three main obstacles stand in the way of those who have previously been excluded. The first obstacle is the perception by those who hold power that broader participation is a threat to their interests and, hence, to stability. Second, the fragility of emerging institutions representing the interests of those who have so long been excluded is also an obstacle. Finally, the fact that the excluded are often the poorest in society, and therefore have fewer financial resources for mobilizing as a political force, stands as another major obstacle.

The international community can be extremely helpful in supporting broader political participation of domestic groups. Because democracy is a key objective of Esquipulas II, and because all Central American governments have ratified the American Convention on Human Rights, there is a legitimate and compelling basis for inducing Central American governments to adhere to democratic principles. The requirements (or "conditionality") imposed on loans, other financial arrangements, or even political and diplomatic interaction with the Central American leaders, can address the observance of democratic practice without overstepping the bounds of noninterference. Since extra-regional powers hold the key to financing Central America's economic recovery, economic conditionality is discussed at length in Chapter 6.

As long as international assistance is in keeping with the noninterference stipulations of the Esquipulas II accords, Central American governments should recognize the right of nongovernmental groups to seek support of the broader regional and international communities. International funding and training can help to overcome the disparities in resources and skills that put groups representing the poor at a disadvantage. Affiliation with regional or international movements can help insulate local groups from political exclusion or repression. Because regional and international connections enhance a local group's ability to communicate its situation to the outside world, civil rights violations are more likely to be visible internationally, and to bring censure upon the violators.

Democracy can also be broadened within government through decentralization. Local government is the training ground for national participation. A local government with real authority over development decisions, as long as it is not dominated by local elites, can bring democracy home to previously nonparticipating or excluded people. Even the poorest populations can become directly involved in local development issues. Thus financial decentralization, which is often advisable out of considerations of administrative efficiency, deepens democracy.

Tolerance: Human Rights

Respect for human rights is fundamental to democracy. Few challenges are more difficult for democratic development than enforcing human rights laws and prosecuting human rights violations, yet disregard for human rights violates all individuals' integrity as human beings and citizens. Moreover, world experience has shown that repression through human rights violations often breeds greater discontent, heightens social conflict, and undermines the legitimacy of a political system.

For democracy to prevail, military and civilian courts must expand the prosecution of human rights violations. Improved training and discipline within the armed forces and police can help uphold professional military standards and curb human rights abuses by the military.

Governments must also assure the independence and physical security of judicial personnel—especially judges and lawyers. The autonomy of the judiciary means that its members must be free to reach decisions independently, without being influenced by other branches of government or the military. For this to be possible, the judicial branch requires control over the financial resources necessary to carry out its functions and control over its own personnel. Through both training and financial support to strengthen legal systems, international aid can again be extremely helpful.

The regional and international communities can also support the work of human rights organizations, church-supported human rights groups, and local and national programs offering legal services. The Central American Court of Justice, a new judicial body described in Chapter 5, could help resolve disputes that arise between the Central American nations or between regional institutions.

International institutions, such as the Inter-American Commission on Human Rights and the Inter-American Court of Human Rights, have played crucial roles in supporting human rights. These organizations should be accorded an increased role in monitoring human rights observance. Domestic groups operating under the protection of Catholic and Protestant churches have also played a critical role in monitoring human rights abuses in the region. They have provided legal and humanitarian services to political prisoners and their families and to the families of the disappeared. They also raise the visibility of human rights violations nationally and internationally.

Tolerance: Instilling Values of Democracy and Peace

After decades of mutual suspicion and open conflict, Central Americans have little basis for mutual trust or for confidence in democracy. Democratic norms have to be cultivated. This is one of the virtues of the Central American Parliament, discussed in the chapter on regional cooperation.

To directly instill these democratic values, the Commission proposes the creation of a Cultural and Educational Council. This body would be dedicated to the exchange of information, knowledge, and technology on the development of human resources among the five Central American countries in support of the principles of democracy, peace, and development. Because the tradition of peace and democracy has been absent in Central America outside of Costa Rica, instilling commitment to these principles must go beyond formal practices and the absence of armed conflict. The aspiration in the region for peace, democracy and development stems in part from a frustration with the sacrifices of war and does not yet rest on deeply rooted cultural values of respect for democracy and the love of peace. Without developing such values, no new development strategy or structure will function well in the long run.

To this end, the Cultural and Educational Council would organize seminars, produce publications, and create education programs, but also serve as a mechanism for ensuring that the process of human resources development truly reinforces peace, democracy, and development. The Council would evaluate human resource development programs, projects, and educational efforts and would verify that they are properly targeted and effective.

The Cultural and Educational Council would also provide a window to absorb new financial and technical assistance from the international community for the explicit purpose of human resources development in support of peace and democracy.

The key to structuring the Cultural and Educational Council is to integrate national, regional, and international interactions. On the national levels, the participation of government, labor, cooperatives, the private sector, nongovernmental organizations, and other organized groups would demonstrate that democracy and tolerance are not mere slogans. On the regional level, as with the Central American Parliament, democratic practices of one country can reinforce those of the others. Internationally, the recognition of the Cultural and Educational Council would signal an endorsement of the practical utility of peaceful cooperation.

Civilian Rule and Civil-Military Relations

Central American governments must engage the armed forces in the movement toward democracy. The armed forces have an essential and legitimate role in protecting the security of each Central American nation. But security is not achieved by repression and military dominance of government. Continued withdrawal of the military from the political scene, their training in democratic political values, the rejection of authoritarian doctrines of national security, and the development of effective mechanisms of civilian political control are indispensable elements for achieving the demilitarization of Central American societies.

METHODIST COLLEGE LIBRARY
FAYETTEVILLE, NC

Nevertheless, in light of the military's heavy current involvement in governance as well as security, the Commission recommends that the civilian and military leaders engage in an institutional dialogue on the issue of reforming civil-military relations. The emphasis of these discussions must be on cooperation—rather than open confrontation—between civilians and the armed forces. Civilian leaders and the armed forces must jointly define a democratic concept of security, military professionalism and international military cooperation to assure that the armed forces contribute to the consolidation and protection of democracy, peace, and development.

Disengagement. The fact that Costa Rica, El Salvador, Guatemala, and Honduras have civilian presidents indicates that the armed forces have made a provisional commitment to the process of democratization. Concerted action toward peace also will tend to reduce the armed forces' reluctance to disengage politically. But if the militaries are to be expected to accept further withdrawal from political control, it is essential for extra-regional and intra-regional support of insurgencies to end.

Dealing with Civilian Governments on Security Issues. Civilian control over relationships with extra-regional security forces is also essential. Extra-regional powers have sometimes bypassed civilian authorities to deal directly with the Central American armed forces because of the attraction of engaging the institution with the highest presumed commitment to security and counter-insurgency.

If extra-regional governments deal with the Central American armed forces as professional institutions subordinate to civilian control, then the civilian authorities would be in a better position to assert responsible control. The massive flows of military assistance coming into Central America give extra-regional powers enormous potential to induce the Central American armed forces to adhere to democratic principles and play a professionalized, nonpolitical role.

Promoting the Professionalism of the Military. Despite the leadership and sacrifices that some military personnel have shown over the past decades, some elements of the armed forces have been drawn into political entanglements and corruption that have diverted them from achieving the professional status for which military officers are trained and to which many aspire. Democratic development that is not seen as a threat to the military's institutional survival can carry the armed forces toward the status of the respected and professionalized militaries of North America and Western Europe. Several

South American militaries have moved successfully in this direction.

Ultimately, the reduction of arms will enable the channeling of resources away from military programs and into economic and social development. The reduction of military budgets is imperative, yet it has to be paced so that the security risks do not increase significantly, and it must be sensitive to the importance of adequate military salaries for encouraging and maintaining a professional orientation within the armed forces. Low salaries, as much as lack of professionalism, have induced the forays of military officers into private business affairs and to the use of political power for personal gain.

Economic and Social Justice

Bringing Central Americans now living in poverty into the economic mainstream is just as important as engaging the military in the movement toward political freedom and democracy. In the short run, this means nurturing a wide range of institutions that foster broad-based social and economic participation. Over the long run, institutions such as political parties, unions, cooperatives, nongovernmental organizations, and church groups help increase the capacities of currently marginal groups to participate more fully.

As stressed in the third chapter of this report, a human resources strategy is essential to promote wider and more active participation of the entire population. Among the groups traditionally excluded from social and economic justice are women, indigenous groups, workers, and the rural and urban poor. The Commission's human resources strategy emphasizes the importance of investing in basic needs as well as reforming policy to equalize access to credit and employment for these Central Americans. Wider opportunities for literacy and primary education, in particular, will promote both economic and political development.

Strengthening political parties throughout Central America is another important method for widening social participation. One serious weakness of the region's political parties is their tendency to split into factions, divided by ideology, personality, and mutual intolerance. This factionalization of parties and movements damages the effectiveness of their programs and organizations.

Nongovernmental Organizations. The international community can promote democratic development by supporting institutions that foster economic and social justice. Growing worldwide involvement through international nongovernmental organizations has already been a tremendous help to Central Americans. During the 1980s crisis, more than 100 nongovernmental organizations have begun working in the region, contributing an estimated $200 million in aid to Central America in 1987 alone.

The growth of international NGOs was accompanied by rapid expansion of a network of approximately 600 local counterparts—called local development organizations—that now benefit over 5 million Central Americans. NGOs have become key players in promoting the development capacity of broad sectors of society. They have great potential for assisting in the recovery and development of Central America.

The Esquipulas II accords provided NGOs with an opportunity to become more actively involved in the current transition period to lay the bases for democracy and development through popular participation in the integration process. Critical tasks of repatriation, economic and social relocation of refugees, and reconstruction have already begun, administered and coordinated by nongovernmental organizations and their local counterparts even amid persisting conflict.

Nongovernmental organizations have the potential to multiply their efforts. National and international NGOs have provided training for millions of Central American citizens. In addition, through international contacts, nongovernmental organizations have helped transfer appropriate technologies and skills for development. Finally, NGOs can help to develop the productive capacity of the informal sector, overseeing welfare and distributive policies where governments have had little effect, and fostering the informal sector's capacity for development.

However, governments should not take advantage of the existence of NGOs to shirk governmental responsibilities to deliver social services. At both national and regional levels, governments should engage in dialogue with NGOs and local development organizations to establish their role in national and regional projects and to coordinate the best use of the region's resources.

Democracy and Elections

Elections are the most obvious and visible element of democracy, although their existence alone does not assure democratic health. The other facets of democracy discussed above are necessary for free and competitive elections.

In recent years, the capacity to judge the fairness of elections has benefited from well-developed mechanisms for the selection of credible election observer teams. Now it is crucial to link the findings of these teams to the international community's judgment of progress toward the Esquipulas objectives.

International party movements face the delicate task of nurturing the democratic development and participation of local parties without undue interference in the domestic politics of each Central American nation. Inevitably, there will be disputes over whether a particular action by the international movement constitutes undue interference, or whether the government is violating the civil rights of the local parties by restricting their actions or those of the international movement. The Central American Parliament and the Central American Court of Justice (which are discussed in the chapter on regional cooperation) can both play an essential role in addressing these disputes.

The Media in Democratic Development. The media can play an extremely useful role in promoting both democracy and development. In much of Central America, however, the media's role is limited and biased. The region's governments, the international community, and Central American newspeople can help improve the impact of television, radio, and print journalism on democratic development.

In general, Central American media tend to be dominated by the elite, leaving the majority with little access to the major channels of communication. Media coverage also tends to be skewed to urban centers. Laws protecting freedom of information and the press have often been limited or ignored, and the fear of repression—through intimidation, closure, exile, and even assassination—has sharply diminished willingness to engage in open questioning or debate.

By encouraging critical debate, governments can do much to enhance the public's understanding of critical national issues and its participation in decisionmaking. National governments, however, do a great disservice to democracy if they block the free operation of independent media. Governments must also help guarantee the physical security of newspeople and citizens who express their opinions.

The media can also strengthen its contribution to society. By placing greater emphasis on educational programs—including agriculture, health, literacy, culture, and the conservation of natural resources—and by broadening its coverage, the media can better contribute to the process of broad-based Central American development.

As long as international involvement does not violate the norms of noninterference set forth in the Esquipulas accords, financial assistance and advanced training from the international community can be a great help to Central American media. By providing the financing to recruit and train talented newspeople from different backgrounds, the international community can help offset urban, elite biases. International financial aid can also help overcome the limits, imposed by scarce resources, on developing locally based media.

Chapter 5

Revitalizing Regional Integration

Regional cooperation is essential to Central American development, not only to revive the economies but also to enhance the peace process. Once the catalyst for strong regional development, the Central American Common Market holds great potential for the recovery and development of the entire region. But integration must go far beyond a market for regional trade to include broad economic and political cooperation. For this type of cooperation to be successful, however, efforts must address the difficult problems that hindered former attempts and must adapt to the challenges of changed local and regional conditions.

As the primary implementors of economic integration, the regional institutions created in the early 1960s should once again catalyze and guide Central American integration. Under the leadership of the five national governments, these institutions could reduce tensions within the region and strengthen the process of national democratization. In a new strategy for integration, regional institutions can provide numerous channels for interchange among nations even when bilateral relations are strained. Yet this will not be possible unless the regional institutions are substantially revamped.

Although war and economic crisis have severely weakened regional institutions, they are basically intact and could be renewed and redirected toward forging a new postwar strategy for integration and regional development. If they are backed by clear political direction and sufficient financial and technical support, regional institutions can once again play a crucial role in planning, coordinating, and implementing regional efforts.

Since the Esquipulas II accords, the Central Americans have made an extraordinary effort to coordinate their actions and proposals. This interchange, ranging from meetings of the presidents and vice-presidents to regional conclaves of private associations, reflects the enthusiasm for integration. Furthermore, it has also identified some of the bases for institutionalizing this coordination on the government-to-government level.

In the political realm, the five foreign ministers have assumed some direct responsibility for advancing the peace process. The Executive Committee of the Vice-Presidents has undertaken to negotiate on behalf of the region and oversees the international aspects of regional integration involving international financial institutions, multilateral organizations such as the European Community and the Nordic Community, and regional programs like the Caribbean Basin Initiative and the Montevideo Treaty. Reinforced by the treaty establishing the Central American Parliament, these functions should also be strengthened and supported internationally.[49]

The primary structure for economic coordination consists of the ministers responsible for economic integration.[50] With the support of the central banks and the ministers of finance, these ministers operate in conjunction with Sectoral Councils (composed of ministers of agriculture, energy, transportation, and other departments).

The Democratic Potential of Regional Integration

One of the most important contributions of regional institutions is their role in supporting democratic change throughout Central America. Two kinds of regional arrangements can contribute directly to the advancement of democracy in Central America. First, region-wide movements like political parties, organized labor, the media, cooperatives, entrepreneurs, and nongovernmental organizations can find strength in regional solidarity if any government tries to infringe on their legitimate rights. As reviewed in Chapter 4, these movements should enhance civil society's capacity to participate in building peace and democracy.

Political parties' participation in the region's integration process, for example, is essential for overcoming the skepticism toward integration found in some circles. If apprised of the new integration strategies, the parties can help forge a regional political will. Through the assistance and protection that regionalism can offer the parties' national affiliates, the same reciprocal relationship among other national movements and corresponding regional ones can greatly support democratic change across Central America.

By establishing democratic patterns that could take hold on the national as well as regional level, official regional institutions are a second type of Central American arrangement that can bolster democracy. The election of deputies to a regional body like the Central American Parliament, for example, can reinforce political parties' participation in domestic politics. The continued exercise of democratic practices like negotiation and open multilateral dialogue in the Parliament could further bolster democracy in each country.

The Central American Parliament, now being established,[51] will be the regional body for contributing to a peaceful environment, promoting the establishment of stable democracies, and overseeing the diplomatic aspects of economic and political integration. It is a decisive step in the institutional growth and consolidation of Central American integration. The Parliament will provide the legitimacy and political framework for debate, even if debate is not sufficiently free in specific countries. The Parliament will also help to overcome political polarization and provide psychological and moral support to the region's fragile democracies.

The Parliament could provide critical support to the International Verification Committee in charge of monitoring the peace processes.[52] It could also support the monitoring of human rights violations, reinforce cooperation among political parties, and play a critical role in supporting efforts toward regional disarmament and in strengthening the civilian character of the national governments. The Commission recommends that the international community provide financial assistance for the establishment of the Central American Parliament.

The Central American Economic and Social Council is another institution that could contribute to the advancement of democracy. The Commission recommends that this institution, whose creation was proposed most recently by the foreign ministers in October 1987, be composed of representatives of organized labor, the private sector, and nongovernmental organizations, and serve as a regional consultative body of civil society. While organized on the regional level, the Economic and Social Council should provide a regular channel of consultation between each Central American government and the broadest range of national groups. Thus it is intended to strengthen the democratic character of the region by providing a mechanism for direct participation, supported and protected by the regional system.

As the Commission envisions it, the Council would also facilitate coordination among public and private groups (including business, labor, cooperative, academic, indigenous and women's groups, and church organizations), rectifying a major weakness of the earlier integration scheme. In promoting new forms of participation involving public-private cooperation, the Council would also contribute to political pluralism in each country and across the region.

The Central American Court of Justice is another regional institution the Commission proposes for its potential contribution to democracy and justice. The need for a Central American Court of Justice has been widely recognized among the various circles promoting integration, given the need to establish expeditious procedures for resolving conflicts among countries and institutions. The growing number of regional institutions and agreements calls for a juridical body to rule on such matters, in order to mitigate conflict and to find just solutions when they cannot be reached through other institutional mechanisms.

Background of Economic Regional Integration

As summarized in Chapter 3, the formation of the CACM in the early 1960s ushered in an era of impressive economic growth. By the late 1970s, the value of intra-regional trade had jumped to over $1 billion, pushing intra-regional exports from 7 percent to 28 percent of total exports. In the process, economic integration allowed local businesses and industries open access to regional markets and helped promote some growth in extra-regional exports. The growth made possible by the wider regional market led to modernization of Central American industry and infrastructure and to increases in the numbers of professionals, skilled industrial workers, and technical personnel.[53]

Despite these gains, the regional integration process faced a series of difficulties. By the second half of the 1960s, certain members of the Common Market began to express dissatisfaction with the distribution of the costs and benefits of integration. A brief war between Honduras and El Salvador in 1969 further complicated regional relations, leading Honduras to break diplomatic relations with El Salvador and effectively end free trade between the two countries. Having raised concerns over the distribution of the integration process, Honduras pulled out of the common tariff agreement in 1970.

The sharp and continuing drop in intra-regional trade after 1980 was exacerbated by a number of factors including the global recession of the early 1980s, the costs of servicing growing debts, and, above all, the outbreak of civil wars. By 1985, the regional trading partners had accumulated deficits totaling almost $600 million. As other Central American governments began to violate the common external tariff and adopt protectionist measures to face the crisis, the value of intra-regional trade fell to less than one-third of its 1980 peak.

The modern industry that had expanded through the integration process, however, was critically dependent on the regional market. The collapse of regional trade left a great deal of productive capacity idle, incurring losses both in overall export levels and in the efficiency of local industry. Furthermore, by the mid-1980s, the physical infrastructure serving regional activities, largely built in the 1960s, was reaching the end of its useful lifetime. Highways, telecommunications facilities, manufacturing plants, and electricity grids were obsolete or badly decaying.

Despite these setbacks, the case for revitalizing Central American trade and economic integration is still strong:

– each Central American market alone is too small to ensure its economic viability;
– in each country, the most dynamic entrepreneurial sector is inextricably linked to regional industrialization;
– the existing productive capacity, built through decades of scarce savings, is vital for Central American economic recovery;
– insertion in international markets depends greatly on gaining the economies of scale and building sufficient competitiveness. These can be enhanced by serving a regional rather than domestic market;
– region-wide programs[54] can establish multiple support services (marketing, transportation, finance, technological research and development, and market research), further encouraging expansion and competitiveness.

In addition to these arguments for reviving regional integration, there are recent signs that regional commerce is growing. Declines in regional trade and cooperation seemed to bottom out in 1987. The Esquipulas II accord represented a very favorable diplomatic shift, and in that same year intra-regional trade increased by $73 million, the first increase since the advent of the crisis. This was due in part to external financial cooperation and the coordinated increase in the central banks' foreign exchange reserves.

Challenges to Renewed Economic Integration

While there are clear advantages to revitalizing Central American trade, there are also major challenges. For broad economic cooperation to be possible, reforms must be undertaken to coordinate and harmonize macroeconomic policies. Reestablishing the common external tariff and the free trade zone depends on Central American leadership and commitment. Equally important, the five nations must address the unequal distribution of the benefits of integration, particularly for Honduras.[55]

Furthermore, the influence of narrowly focused interests must be diminished; institutions for orchestrating regional modernization must be developed; and political support for reforming the structure and programs of existing regional organizations must be increased. There are external challenges to integration that must also be addressed, ranging from problems of servicing the external debt to the dominance of bilateral over regional relations (see Chapter 6).

In sum, economic reconstruction and development will revolve primarily around a set of regional schemes: reestablishing the free trade zone and the common external tariff; restructuring regional economic growth through policy coordination and investment; and reducing the regional debt burden. New institutions and programs will be needed as the renewed integration process takes hold.

Rebuilding the Free Trade Zone. Regional trade must be revitalized while providing strong incentives to promote exports to global markets. Protection must not be a shelter for inefficient and monopolistic industrial production. The common external tariff providing limited and declining protection should be reestablished. A target of a 30 percent maximum regional tariff, reached over a period of five to seven years, is a realistic goal.

By approving a new common tariff agreement in 1984, the Central American countries have taken a giant step forward in revising and reestablishing the Common External Tariff. Though Honduras has preferred to remain outside the regional framework for matters of trade, the new Honduran tariff schedule does not include any fundamental discrepancies with the common tariff. As a result, rebuilding the Central American customs union is feasible.

The common tariff policy, however, faces opposition from certain sectors of the five countries as well as the international community. The conditionality of sectoral and structural adjustment programs of the World Bank, the IMF, and the U.S. Agency for International Development seems to be designed to decrease the extent of protectionism on an exclusively national basis, without concern for regional consistency. Crisis conditions have led the governments to make unilateral tariff changes from time to time, which then give rise to reprisals by other Central American governments. As the result greatly complicates efforts at regional economic integration, the Commission recommends stopping these practices.

Coordination of National Economic Policies. A minimum level of convergence of macroeconomic policies is essential if integration is to succeed.[56] The Commission recommends that governments, regional institutions, multilateral financial institutions, and bilateral development agencies work to encourage the convergence of domestic policies.

Restoring a full free trade area will involve closer coordination of monetary and exchange rate policy among all countries of the region. The common tariff must be reinforced by realistic and stable exchange rate policies, aiming for a unified, market rate. If governments feel compelled to adopt a dual system instead of a unified rate, the difference between the two rates should not exceed 25 percent.

Such actions require flexibility and pragmatism to ensure that the rebuilding process does not fail because of excessively ambitious or rigid arrangements. Special short-term trade arrangements must be planned to ensure that creditor countries do not incur onerous imbalances. Central Americans must also resolve the special case of Nicaragua, whose involvement is critical for recapturing regional economic growth.

Clearly, Nicaragua must undertake a stabilization program to eliminate distortions in prices relative to the other Central American economies. Involving Nicaragua more fully requires not only special arrangements to improve its financial status, but also serious adjustment measures to make its economy more compatible (in inflation rates and exchange policies, for example) with the other four countries. Nonetheless, trade with Nicaragua can be increased through a financial program that includes support from the surplus countries.[57]

Generating Investment Programs. There is ample room for regional cooperation in promoting new exports. Coordination of the international community's cooperation in investment programs designed by SIECA, ICAITI and CABEI could greatly enhance the results.[58] Central American agricultural producers have called for research and development programs to increase the variety and quality of new agricultural export products.[59] Aggressive marketing services should receive regional support, particularly if they include the complementary services of finance, transportation, and marketing.

Intra-Regional Debt is a major obstacle to economic integration. Restoration of intra-regional trade requires rehabilitating a payment-clearing mechanism that permits use of national currencies for exchange rather than dollars.

A necessary first step is to eliminate the $722 million of intra-regional debts. The second step must be the creation of mechanisms to prevent such imbalances from accumulating so that deficit countries can undertake needed modifications in policy. Creditor countries must be prepared to write off some part of existing debt, and debtor countries to commit themselves to nonprotectionist adjustment policies that will prevent debt recurrence. Of course, the feasibility and durability of these steps also depend on the resolution of Central America's external debt problem, as discussed in Chapter 6.

Lasting solutions to intra-regional debt depend on adequate foreign exchange reserves. Additional foreign exchange in support of the Central American Clearing House would contribute greatly to restore the credibility in intra-regional exchange convertibility, without which trade is reduced to virtual barter and governments would be even more likely to resort to protectionist measures in order to balance transactions.

Strengthening Regional Institutions

Though they have suffered from decreased budgets, difficulties in attracting qualified personnel, and diminished political support by member governments, the region's specialized economic institutions should once again lead efforts toward integration.

Even in the midst of crisis and polarization, the Secretariat of the Treaty of Central American Economic Integration (SIECA), the Central American Bank for Economic Integration (CABEI), the Central American Monetary Council, and the Central American Clearing House all played important roles in proposing and implementing policies to mitigate the crisis and to maintain the structure of integration. Numerous sectoral institutions also contributed to regional integration.[60]

SIECA should be responsible for proposing the strategic guidelines for Central American trade policy and for coordinating the export development program. In the new integration scheme, SIECA should also oversee the technical preparation and the consultations for coordinating national fiscal, monetary, and trade policies. In the shorter term, the difficult technical challenge is to design corrective or compensatory mechanisms to reconcile divergent macroeconomic approaches. SIECA would also coordinate the technical work and the negotiations to gain explicit recognition of the Central American integration zone in the rules of conditionality of multilateral lending agencies.

SIECA will also have to develop compensatory mechanisms for countries with chronic regional trade deficits, as well as coordinate the activities of other integration institutions. Specifically, SIECA should develop strategies for modernizing Central American industry, agriculture, energy policy, transportation, communication, and other basic infrastructure.[61]

Strengthening the *Central American Bank for Economic Integration* (CABEI) would enable the mobilization of resources from Central America and abroad; the design of instruments for capturing savings in hard currencies (and reducing capital flight); and technical support for Central American governments as they renegotiate foreign debts or undertake "swap" operations. CABEI's technical and operational capabilities must be strongly reinforced in planning and evaluation of sectoral projects, coordination of information for domestic financial institutions, loan execution and disbursement, and export-investment promotion. Finally, to make optimal use of the national financial institutions' networks and facilities, CABEI should coordinate the countries' development banks and finance companies in consultation with central banks. This, of course, requires greater support from the five governments. The governments must bring their CABEI contributions up-to-date and display the willingness to allow CABEI to take the lead on financial coordination.

The *Secretariat of the Central American Monetary Council* should join with CABEI in advising the governments on the management, renegotiation, and preparation of special debt operations, and should promote agreements for regional coordination of monetary and exchange rate policies.

The distinctive task of the Monetary Council should be to seek mechanisms for financing intra-regional trade. Accrued balances should be unfrozen by granting credits on concessional terms, or allowing for substantial discounts between central banks. To cover new debts generated while regional trade imbalances are being corrected, external funds should be obtained temporarily to permit expanded commerce. Renewed initiatives for this purpose should be presented to the European Economic Community and other entities to strengthen the Central American Common Market Fund. Also, backed by the Declaration of Acapulco, Central America should request incorporation into the Santo Domingo Agreement.[62]

Acting Together Internationally

Central America must put forth joint proposals on regional priorities as a fundamental prerequisite of the tasks described above. But the international community must also adopt criteria of a multilateral nature and be prepared to negotiate on a multilateral basis. To improve coordination of aid programs, a multilateral and multisectoral forum of lenders and recipients should be established (see the discussion of the Central American Development Coordination Commission in Chapter 6). Another area with great potential for regional cooperation is participation as a regional bargaining unit in the Uruguay Round of negotiations on GATT. In negotiations on regional trade issues and aid for regional projects, the five Central American governments can negotiate as a bloc with counterpart multilateral groups of trading partners or international agencies.[63]

Institutional Coherence

In pointing to the need to strengthen existing institutions and to consider establishing new ones, the Commission recognizes the importance of institutional coherence and the disadvantages of institutional duplication and waste. Therefore the Commission recommends that a comprehensive assessment of the institutional structure of Central American integration be carried out by the governments, representatives of a broad range of social sectors, and those who support these institutions financially. The European Community, with its long experience in developing regional structures, is in an excellent position to provide expertise for this review.

Chapter 6

International Cooperation

Much of this report focuses on actions the Central American nations themselves must take to achieve peace, democracy, and development. The Commission recognizes, however, that the Central American republics are small, poor nations highly sensitive to the actions of outside forces. Central American efforts, therefore, are in danger of being frustrated unless the international community lends its unequivocal support. This support must be manifest in coordinated diplomacy that places peace and democracy on equal footing, and in economic policies that provide Central America with the opportunities for growth with equity.

Esquipulas Conditionality

The world community should give its full and unremitting support to the consolidation of peace and democracy as envisioned by the Esquipulas accords. As an important first step, all nations should undertake a concerted withdrawal of outside military aid to irregular forces and insurrectionary movements.

To give maximum impetus to the peace and democratization process, the Commission recommends that the international community base its relations with Central American states—including diplomatic, economic, cultural, and security arrangements—on their compliance with the Esquipulas accords. By the same token, the Commission strongly urges that countries in compliance with the guidelines of Esquipulas not be denied financial assistance or trade benefits on the basis of other political criteria.

Currently, the Esquipulas verification mechanism consists of certification of progress by the Central American presidents and monitoring by a multilateral verification body. In support of the Esquipulas process, the Commission recommends that the international community establish a collaborative, consultative process for sharing information and evaluating progress toward peace and democracy. In order for these criteria to be applied with the greatest possible consistency, the international community should take into account the advice of this collaborative body in determining how to relate to the Central American governments.

Reinforcing Regional Structures

For Central America to be able to act as a region, it must be treated as a region. For the Central American governments to join forces to pursue peace, democracy, and development, they must be able to rely on international processes that bring them together. International diplomacy can place its leverage behind the region's inherent tendencies toward integration and help to diminish centrifugal forces that could tear the region apart.

The regional initiatives outlined in Chapter 5 require international support —financial and political. Donors should help to finance the revival of the Common Market and the creation of other regional institutions such as the Central American Parliament and the Cultural and Educational Council. The international community should also validate regional initiatives and strengthen Central American regional institutions by having them participate in deliberations and negotiations over such issues as regional security, aid, trade, debt, and environmental planning.

International Economic Cooperation: Trade and Technology

A healthy, global economy, with low interest rates, firm commodity prices, and expanding trade, would provide a favorable environment for Central American development. Thus, Central America has a strong stake in the effective coordination of macroeconomic policies by the industrialized nations. In addition, the revival of the region's economies depends heavily on the openness of external markets, the availability of modern technology, and on the restructuring of old debts and the inflow of new capital.

In this regard, improvements in Central America's investment climate will encourage direct investment from industrialized nations.

Opening Markets for Central American Exports

For the long-term development of the region, trade is more important than aid. The export-promotion strategy can succeed only to the extent that other countries reduce their tariffs and increase the quotas on Central American exports.

The heavy Central American dependence on a handful of export products, whose value has dropped precipitously, was an important cause of the region's overall economic decline. Therefore the Commission's proposed development strategy highlights concerted efforts to broaden and diversify Central American exports. But without the cooperation of industrialized nations and the more advanced Latin American countries, serious diversification will remain limited by the risks involved in investing in export initiatives without secure market opportunities.

Despite requests by Central American governments, the international community has not been forthcoming in granting broader market access. One exception is the Caribbean Basin Initiative (CBI), which has stimulated some export expansion into the U.S. market. The CBI, however, is limited in scope and in time, creating doubts that trade openings will be long-lasting enough to warrant the investment risks.[64] Costa Rica, whose manufactured goods constitute nearly half of all manufactured exports from Central America, is the only country in the region to have realized significant benefits so far.

To fulfill the potential of the CBI, the Commission urges the U.S. government to extend it beyond the original 12-year term and expand its terms to provide opportunities for critical items—most importantly textiles and apparel, which make up 60 percent of Central America's manufactured exports and hold strong growth potential.

The Commission recommends that similar initiatives be developed and coordinated by other industrialized nations, including the Nordic countries, Canada, Japan, and the European Community which now buys one-fourth of all Central American exports. Since total Central American exports represent an extremely small proportion of world trade, and the output levels of Central America's agricultural and industrial sectors are very low compared to the economies of large countries, the costs of lowering trade barriers will be modest—while Central America could benefit greatly.

In light of Central America's severe crisis and its commitment to rebuilding its economies, the Commission calls on the international community to grant unilateral trade concessions and to remove all tariff barriers to Central American exports for at least 10 years. Where quotas exist, Central America should receive preferential treatment. This would apply to agricultural commodities such as sugar, beef, and coffee, as well as to such manufactured items as garments, textiles, and shoes.

Reviving Intra-Regional Trade

The international community can support the Central American leaders in revitalizing intra-regional trade, both by recognizing and supporting the Central American priority of regional economic integration, and by helping to remove the obstacles to reviving regional trade.

Reconstruction of a system of economic cooperation will require a substantial amount of new money. Imaginative arrangements are essential for settling the debts that have accumulated through intra-regional trade (and now total some $722 million), and new funds are required for assuring steady aid inflows in order to make domestic financial reform feasible. Reestablishing a sound trade payments structure will require additional foreign exchange for the Central American Clearing House with outside resources provided on a temporary basis.

Technology Policy

The opening of foreign markets will provide new opportunities for Central American economic expansion, but it will also present the challenges of international competition. To raise levels of productivity and efficiency, to compete effectively, and to develop new products, Central America must acquire advanced technology. The 1980s crisis has had particularly adverse effects on the region's technological progress and has widened the gap between the technology utilized by the most developed countries and the technology applied in Central America. Obtaining modern technology that is compatible with local conditions and resources will be crucial to the region's efforts to increase productivity and efficiency.

The increasing costs of sophisticated technology, coupled with the shortage of financial resources in Central America, make international assistance essential. International support could take at least five forms: the exchange of scientists and researchers, the supply of equipment and materials, joint ventures in research and development, preferential license and patent arrangements, and direct financial assistance. In addition, multinational corporations can be a potent source of technology; in Central America, joint ventures are often an especially convenient arrangement for the transfer of technology. The Central American Institute for Industrial Research (ICAITI) would be an appropriate channel for such international support.

Financial Flows: Annual Requirements

To devote resources to the revitalization of trade and the implementation of domestic reforms, Central American countries must be assured adequate external financial assistance. Too often, drastic monetary devaluations and reductions in tariff protection have been part of short-term measures designed to deal with balance-of-payments emergencies. The results have not been successful. If capital inflows are assured, central banks can use reserves to reduce speculation and gain credibility for new policies. Moreover, adequate capital flows help governments compensate those groups who suffer from adjustment measures, thereby reducing opposition to desirable reforms and making them more politically feasible.

Although the Commission is not proposing massive increases in external capital flows into Central America, continued aid and financial assistance are essential. The current level of financial resources flowing into the region is estimated at approximately $1.5 billion. The Commission urges the international community to increase the net external financial flows from the current levels to $2 billion per year for the next five years. Of the $2 billion annual flows, at least $850 million should be devoted for each of the first three years to meet urgent needs, focusing largely on refugees and displaced persons.

The figure of $2 billion per year is based on calculations of the net inflows necessary for a gradual recuperation to a sustainable growth path of 5.5 percent by 1993. This assumes that debts will be restructured—a step that is particularly essential to improving the prospects of Costa Rica and Nicaragua.[65] In the absence of new debt arrangements, the total bill would increase to $2.5 billion annually to keep pace with scheduled interest payments. The largest per capita requirements correspond to Nicaragua, El Salvador, and Honduras.

The target growth rate of 5.5 percent by 1993 will not even bring Central America back to its 1980 levels of per capita income except in Costa Rica. However, the rigidities in the Central American economies (even with the sound economic policies presumed by the Commission's projections) and the need to base sustainable growth on sound investments preclude absorbing capital more rapidly. The 5.5 percent growth target is a healthy and feasible objective; an effort to absorb more than the $2 billion net external inflow would lead to massive waste and to even greater financial burdens.

Debt Reduction and Restructuring

In the 1980s, all Central American countries have suffered a sharp decline in their terms of trade. With the added financial strains of war and the deterioration of intra-regional trade, total exports in the region fell from $4.6 billion in 1979 to $3.8 billion in 1987. As export growth and economic activity slumped, levels of debt and debt service climbed rapidly. For the region as a whole, debt service payments rose from consuming 12 percent of exports in 1980 to 40 percent in 1987.

Lightening the $18 billion debt burden is therefore another critical step to help Central America recapture its dynamism in this special period of recovery. Through a combination of debt reduction and restructuring, Central America must get relief from the debts it owes, in roughly equal proportions, to private, bilateral, and multilateral sources. Not only will reducing debt service payments diminish the need for foreign assistance, but alleviating the debt burden will also permit the region's governments to enact effective, medium-term adjustment policies. These policies will in turn make sustainable development possible.

For the three types of debt—private, bilateral, and multilateral—the Commission recommends different steps.

(a) *Private bank debt*, already heavily discounted for the most indebted Central American countries, Costa Rica and Nicaragua, should be reduced through its repurchase by the Central American governments through an official funding loan from other nations. This would also be a way of involving the European Community, the Nordic countries, Japan, or others in Central American reconstruction. Substantially reducing the private debt will have few repercussions on potential private bank flows to the region. Done on a case-by-case basis in response to market evaluations and bank recognition of their excess exposure, such a policy enhances future opportunities for sounder lending. Elimination of the present arrears holds out the possibility of increasing short-term commercial bank trade credits in support of expanding exports, a positive element for export promotion.

(b) *Bilateral official debt* should be rescheduled over a multiyear period rather than waiting for the next crisis. This could make foreign exchange reserves more predictable over the span of medium term adjustment. Amortization should be postponed to help avoid the need for new loans to pay off the old and make new investment projects possible. In the case of Nicaragua, because of the size of its official debt, significant reduction is necessary.

(c) For *multilateral debt*, the basic solution lies in an expanded program of inflows that can reverse the negative resource transfers from Central America to multilateral creditors. This requires a multiyear perspective and a positive predisposition toward the region on the part of the multilateral institutions.

Within this framework, the exact modalities of debt restructuring will have to be designed to meet the specific needs of each nation, and negotiated in conjunction with comprehensive programs of structural adjustment. Moreover, debt restructuring should occur in the context of a determination of each nation's overall capital requirements.

These recommendations for reducing and restructuring debt will help ease Central America's foreign exchange problem. But the bulk of needed capital will still have to come from new inflows. As stressed in Chapter 3, the effectiveness of these new flows will be determined largely by each country's commitment to enacting comprehensive programs of structural adjustment.

Foreign Assistance: Diversification and Coordination

The Commission feels that the region would benefit from a diversification of its capital providers. Diversification would allow for increased volume and would reduce the risks of fluctuations in levels and political discrimination in country allocations. The Commission calls upon the United States to maintain its current assistance levels, but it is aware that U.S. budgetary pressures preclude any substantial increases. Fortunately, the trend away from very heavy reliance on U.S. foreign assistance is already under way, but contributions from non-U.S. bilateral donors and from the international financial agencies such as the World Bank and the Inter-American Development Bank should increase in both absolute and relative terms.

This trend to more diversified foreign assistance makes the coordination of aid all the more important and challenging. For this reason, as well as to enhance the evenhandedness of assistance decisions, the Commission calls for the establishment of a multilateral development coordinating mechanism tailored to the unique Central American situation.

A forum such as the Central American Development Coordinating Commission (CADCC) should be created on the principle of symmetrical multilateralism, where donor and recipient countries and international organizations can coordinate aid policies and programs. The CADCC would also foster compliance with regional economic policy, avoid duplication and overlap, minimize gaps in linked development programs, and encourage synergy among programs whenever possible. It would also ensure that international aid, trade, and investment programs are designed and administered in accordance with the objectives of the Esquipulas accords.

Just as the World Bank now provides the umbrella for the coordination of assistance policies in the Caribbean, the Inter-American Development Bank could provide the forum for the CADCC. Within the CADCC, donors and recipients would seek agreement on the broad guidelines for development assistance, while individual nations could meet with their respective donors in Consultative Groups. Country Consultative Groups would formulate bilateral programs consistent with CADCC's overall design.

The operations of the CADCC would in itself be an exercise in democracy, involving social partners from each of the donor and recipient countries. Therefore the CADCC, like the Cultural and Educational Council (see Chapter 3), should include representatives from unions, business, cooperatives, nongovernmental organizations, and other groups.

Economic Conditionality

In addition to conditionality related to progress toward peace and democracy, there is also the more typical conditionality based on economic performance or policy reform.

Governments and international financial institutions impose conditions on aid and loans. Conditionality is inevitable; what matters is its form and objectives. Appropriate conditionality encourages short-term actions that fit within a longer-term time frame of renewed and sustainable growth. It is directed at ensuring consistent and coherent policy rather than insisting on only one narrowly defined development path. It is sensitive to the special circumstances and history of each nation, is supportive of regional initiatives to build cooperation and coordination, and is sensitive to the need to ameliorate the absolute poverty in the region. Finally, because of the commonality of interests among Central American nations and the international community, conditionality can and should be reached through consultations based on mutual respect. It is essential that these conditions reinforce rather than hinder regional integration.

Concluding Statement

In the climate of freedom that democracy ensures, the Central American countries shall make decisions to accelerate development in order to achieve societies that are more egalitarian and free from poverty. Consolidation of democracy involves the establishment of an economy of well-being and an economic and social democracy. To reach those objectives, the governments shall jointly make arrangements to obtain special economic assistance from the international community. —Presidents' agreements, Esquipulas II, August 1987

The principal focus of this report—a development strategy that builds upon Central America's demonstrated economic strengths to reduce poverty and unleash the productive capacity of the region's human resources—goes far beyond improving the lot of the poor and displaced; it goes to the heart of national security and democratic stability in each country. By focusing on efficiency and productivity, the Commission recognizes that poverty alleviation in small countries requires overall growth. By focusing at the same time on the problems of the poorest, the strategy addresses one of the root causes of the unrest of the past decade. Outside support may have fanned the flames of civil unrest, but internal conditions started the fires.

The Commission's appeal to North America, Latin America, Western Europe, and Japan is intimately concerned with the survival of democracy in Central America. The Commission is not calling for enormous new sums of money, but a long-term commitment to support the strategy through trade, aid, and credit, based on progress toward the Esquipulas objectives of peace and democracy. The hope is that the strategy proposed in this report will become a framework that Central American countries and the international community alike can adopt and adapt over the long term.

The recommendations of this Commission, based on the principles of democratic development, are intended to assist Central American leaders in attaining the goals they have set for their societies. Central Americans established these goals, and Central Americans must continue to provide the leadership in achieving them. Foreign aid, credit, and trade concessions are supportive measures; they cannot substitute for the efforts of Central America's leaders to enact difficult policy reforms and to bring essential social services to the poor and to help them become more productive in modern society. The Central American presidents must follow through on their commitment to solve these problems.

The emphasis on developing the human resources of the region, the cornerstone of the Commission's recommendations, has important precedents. As John F. Kennedy stated in 1961, ending poverty was at the heart of the vision of the Alliance for Progress:

> The living standards of every American family will be on the rise, basic education will be available to all, hunger will be a forgotten experience, the need for massive outside help will have passed, most nations will have entered a period of self-sustained growth, and though there will be still much to do, every American republic will be the master of its own revolution and its own hope and progress.

The time is right for applying this human resource emphasis. The Central American nations, backed by the international community, have taken first steps toward achieving peace and laying the foundation for postwar Central America. If peace comes soon, Central America will be poised to rekindle the region's economic growth and expand the recent political openings. If the wars continue, the nations will continue their economic decline, even if financial resources flow into Central America to address the indispensable need to help the victims of war.

The economic trajectory of a more peaceful Central America can be positive if difficult domestic policy reforms are made and the international community responds. Although Central America has been going through a brutal downward spiral, the cessation of hostilities would itself eliminate the enormous drag on the Central American economies caused by mass migration of people, the flight of capital, the destruction of crops and roads, the diversion of resources away from productive investment into military budgets, and the abysmal investment climate of a war-torn region.

The prospects for short-term recovery are bolstered by the demonstrated potential of intra-regional and international trade. The Central American Common Market had been responsible for considerable increases in production and regional trade that have sharply declined over the past decade. The resumption of exchange under new conditions would contribute considerably to reviving the entire region.

Long-term, sustainable, equitable development is much more difficult. Central America cannot afford to allow short-term recovery to block the structural reforms needed to incorporate marginal populations, eliminate distortions, and preserve the natural resource endowment.

The most ominous external possibility is that when Central American wars end and the region is no longer an area of geopolitical crisis, economic aid will be withdrawn and openings for Central American exports closed off. It would be an enormous tragedy if Central America's search for peace were to condemn the region to economic stagnation and eventually another cycle of violence. Recovery, especially if it centers on refugee resettlement and restoration of the region's shattered services infrastructure, will be expensive, though not far beyond the current levels of resources flowing into Central America. Sustained development will require a decade of sustained international support and encouragement.

The Commission approaches the problems of the region with hope and confidence, for even in the past five years, much has changed. One of the most remarkable developments of the modern era is that Central America, despite the turmoil of the past decade, has experienced progress toward democracy. There could be no better testimony to the desire of Central American citizens for a new and more responsive social order than the overwhelming participation in elections, even in countries where voters risked violence.

And once elected, the leaders of the region put aside many of the differences among their countries and joined forces to draft an accord for peace, development, and democracy in Central America. The accords of Esquipulas II is a remarkable vehicle for the difficult task of focusing regional and international efforts on constructive interaction rather than interference.

As a result, the Commission, unlike any that has gone before it, has had the opportunity to forge a set of proposals as a response to the challenge put forward by the leaders of the region. Moreover, the Commission represents no one country or government, but the consensus of 47 citizens from 20 countries, led by a diverse group of Central Americans. The strategy is designed to support the leaders of the region and the democracies they hope to build and preserve. We ask those concerned about the future of Central America to support that goal.

Notes

1. See the text of the Esquipulas accords in Appendix 3.

2. Although these tariffs were high by today's free-trade standards, they were only moderate by Latin American standards of the time.

3. According to the UN Economic Commission for Latin America, *Notas sobre la evolución del desarrollo social del istmo centroaméricano hasta 1980* (México, 1982), p. 153, the bottom two deciles received 4.9 percent of the national income in Guatemala in 1970 and 5.3 percent in 1980; the bottom half received 17.4 percent in 1970 and 19.8 percent in 1980. The comparable changes in Honduras were 3.0 to 4.3 percent and 10.7 to 17.0 percent in El Salvador, 3.7 to 2.0 percent and 18.6 to 12.0 percent; in Costa Rica, 5.4 to 4.0 percent and 20.9 to 21.0 percent; in Nicaragua, the bottom half went from 15.0 to 16.0 percent.

4. *CEPAL Review Number 38*, p. 19.

5. Cotton production, however, leads to higher job creation than subsistence crops.

6. Fundación FADES, *Hacia una política de empleo en Centroamérica*, Guatemala, April 1988.

7. María Gallardo and José López, *Centroamérica: La crisis en cifras* (San José, Costa Rica: IICA and FLASCO, 1986), p. 189.

8. Guatemala is the only economy with some oil export capacity.

9. This has occurred in countries where women are traditionally disadvantaged and where a very large percentage of children already receive insufficient nourishment.

10. See Esquipulas II accords in Appendix 3 of this report.

11. See UNDP Special Programme, p. 35.

12. Data on malnutrition taken from the Pan American Health Organization (PAHO), "Priority Health Needs in Central America and Panamá," p. 15; and INCAP/PAHO, "Programas Alimentarios Nacionales," Documentos Técnicos No. 8, Reproducciónes, Buenos Aires, June 1986, section 5. The medical phrase "at risk of malnutrition" is used to indicate a less severe degree of malnutrition; individuals do not get sufficient nutritional value from their food, but are not severely malnourished.

13. The percentage of people with access to safe water varies from 68 percent in Costa Rica to only 18 percent in Guatemala. See the joint paper by the Organization of American States/Inter-American Development Bank/Pan American Health Organization, "Plan for Social Investments in Central America Basic Document," 1987.

14. From interviews conducted by Dr. Segundo Montes for a study of Salvadoran refugees: "El Salvador 1986: en busca de soluciónes para los desplazados," San Salvador, Instituto de Investigaciónes de la Universidad Centroamericana "José Simeón Cañas," 1986.

15. Data is taken from the Fundación Salvadoreña de Desarrollo y Vivienda Mínima (FUNDASAL), El Salvador.

16. Although all of those living in extreme poverty are not starving, they are not getting enough food or even the right foods, and they suffer from high rates of intestinal infections. The extent of poverty as well as the real income levels marking the poverty line vary considerably among the five countries. The average income for the poorest 20 percent of the population, for example, varies substantially. In Costa Rica average 1980 per capita income for the poorest 20 percent of the population was $176 per year; in El Salvador it was $47, and in Honduras $81. (See Economic Commission for Latin America and the Caribbean, 1983.) In all nations of the region poverty is significantly worse in rural areas than in urban ones.

17. See the Proyecto Regional Para la Superación de la Pobreza RLA/86/004, "Bases Para una Estrategia y un Programa de Acción Regional," July 1988.

18. This concern will be addressed by the May 1989 Conference on Central American Refugees, convened by the Central American and Mexican governments and organized by the UN High Commission for Refugees in collaboration with other agencies of the UN system, particularly the UN Development Programme.

19. This estimate is drawn from data gathered by the International Committee for Migration (ICM), PAHO, and from interviews and studies conducted by Dr. Montes, "El Salvador 1986."

20. See Table 1 in Appendix 1 at the conclusion of this report.

21. This number is calculated by multiplying the first priority group by 75 percent. This factor is our own estimate based on ECLAC's poverty studies and repatriation data from several sources. Figures on refugees and internally displaced persons are drawn from Sergio Aguayo's chapter in the companion volume, *Central American Recovery and Development* (Durham, N.C.: Duke University Press, 1989).

22. Our estimates are based on the total of those internally displaced persons and those who are likely to return to their places of origin—300,000 Salvadorans, 135,000 Guatemalans, and 120,000 Nicaraguans for a total of 555,000. To these figures we added those Salvadorans, Nicaraguans, and Guatemalans who are presently living in Honduras and Costa Rica and who are unlikely to return to their native countries. We estimate there are roughly 25,000 refugees in Honduras (most of whom are Salvadorans and Nicaraguans) and roughly 100,000 refugees in

Costa Rica (most of whom are Nicaraguan). These total 125,000 people. Thus the overall total is 125,000 plus 555,000, or 680,000.

23. Thus the 680,000 people in group 2 correspond with approximately 510,000 additional people who live in extreme poverty.

24. See Table 3 in Appendix 1. We assume that the target population represents an even cross section of the larger Central American population from which Table 3 is drawn.

25. See appendix to Chapter 6 on absorptive capacity. A number of factors determine an economy's ability to effectively use aid. These include levels of local administrative and management skills, the availability of feasible projects and the stage of infrastructural development (the condition of roadways and communications systems, for example). Channeling too much foreign aid into an economy can cause inflationary pressures, inefficiency, and corruption.

26. Among others, the following project-based international plans have been developed to respond to economic, social, and health needs: the "Health as a Bridge for Peace" project, organized by PAHO in conjunction with all Central American countries in 1983; the "Plan for Social Investment in Central America," initiated by the Organization of American States and supported by the Inter-American Development Bank and PAHO; and the UN's "Special Plan for Economic Cooperation in Central America." Approximately five years ago the European Economic Community and the Nordic countries (particularly Sweden) have also undertaken special regional development assistance initiatives.

27. Rural food provisions have been estimated on the basis of two-thirds of the minimum caloric intake and should not extend beyond the first crop. The general principle has been that of not creating frictions with other members of the host community, while at the same time promoting investment of participants in income-generating programs and reactivating internal markets. In urban areas subsidies for at least one-third of the minimum caloric intake could be provided through special programs such as food stamps. The lower figure in urban areas reflects that it is far easier to acquire at least some food in urban areas, whereas peasants in removed rural areas may well be unable to get any food until the first crop is harvested. Also, urban programs are longer than rural programs; the former lasting for three years and the latter for only 18 months (thus the net donation is equivalent). Both rural and urban food recipients should progressively decrease their participation in these programs.

28. Programs that provide free food or food in conjunction with work programs should be gradually phased out and changed into programs which only subsidize the costs of food for the target population. Finally, these subsidies should also diminish to the point where food is distributed at market rates but with preferential access.

29. See PAHO, "Priority Health Needs," p. 16.

30. Pan American Health Organization, *Health as a Bridge for Peace.* This is a five-year initiative requiring $1 billion in external funds. Approximately $120 million in external funds have been committed for regional health projects thus far, and another $300 million for national health

projects. The remaining unfunded regional projects are also supported by the UN Special Plan.

31. There should be at least one health post per rural community; in urban areas there should be at least one health unit for every 20,000 people.

32. Community-based organizations should coordinate with those providing the services and supplies to set appropriate fees.

33. Temporary, emergency measures could include insuring the safety of water sources within the community perimeter, providing means for transporting potable water to central locations within the community, and constructing temporary reservoirs for water storage. In those locations where safe drinking water systems exist but require repairs, emergency measures should not last longer than three months. Although constructing potable water services in communities where they do not exist may require more than three months, these actions should be considered as immediate, and the emergency provisions should continue until service is established.

34. Foreign assistance through the immediate actions called for in this report will give different levels of benefits to each of the countries. See Table 5 of Appendix 1 for estimates of benefits by country.

35. Progressive and deliberate reduction of protectionism benefits consumers by lowering the prices they have to pay for imports and reduces production costs. As exports expand, they will provide the foreign currency for the purchase of imported inputs. Reduction of protection should result in greater efficiency by stimulating competitive improvements, which in turn will enhance the demand for purely domestic products as the earnings from increased exports are spent. Export-oriented activity generates employment, particularly in nontraditional activities.

36. See "Returns to Education: A Further International Update and Implications," by George Psacharopoulos, *Journal of Human Resources* 20, no. 4 (Fall 1985).

37. The largest and most active nongovernmental regional initiative is the Central American Institute of Business Administration (INCAE), with campuses in Costa Rica and Nicaragua for training in management and policy analysis.

38. Pan American Health Organization, *Health Conditions in the Americas 1981-1984*; World Bank, *World Development Report 1987*.

39. In Central America in general there is one health worker for 4,800 people, and in some countries there is only one doctor for 8,600 people.

40. International Institute for Environment and Development and World Resources Institute, *World Resources 1987* (New York: Basic Books, 1987), p. 248.

41. Psacharopoulos, "Returns to Education: A Further International Update and Implications."

42. In 1985, only 13 percent of university students in Honduras were women, 11 percent in Nicaragua, 9 percent in El Salvador, and 6 percent in Guatemala. See the chapter by Sally Yudelman in the companion volume to this report, *Central American Recovery and Development*.

43. In Guatemala the World Bank reported 40 percent productivity growth for small investments. According to USAID "PISCES Study," loans in Costa Rica produced income increases of 96 percent after six months and 146 percent after a year. The repayment record also has been excellent. On loans as small as $12 to $300, repayment rates averaged 95 percent. In El Salvador, repayment rates have been as high as 99 percent.

44. In El Salvador the bank oversight board has already instituted a requirement that at least two percent of a commercial bank's own resources go to micro-enterprises.

45. See the chapter by Gustavo Arcia in the companion volume to this report, *Central American Recovery and Development*.

46. See Malcolm Gillis, ed., *Tax Reform in Developing Countries* (Durham, N.C.: Duke University Press, 1989).

47. H. Jeffrey Leonard, *Natural Resources and Economic Development in Central America* (New Brunswick, N.J.: Transaction Books, 1987), introduction.

48. It is significant that the Costa Rican economy, with more developed banking and other credit institutions and more equitable systems of taxation, agricultural policy and industrial policy, responded most vigorously to the export openings afforded by the U.S. Caribbean Basin Initiative. See Stuart Tucker's paper on the Caribbean Basin Initiative in the companion volume to this report, *Central American Recovery and Development*.

49. At present an interinstitutional group constituted by SIECA, CABEI, the Central American Monetary Council, and the Economic Commission for Latin America and the Caribbean has been in charge of preparing studies evaluating the mechanisms mentioned and such plans as the Central American Governments' Plan for Immediate Action. See the Treaty Establishing the Central American Parliament and other political entities, Guatemala, October 2, 1987.

50. This committee has been reconfirmed as the economic arm of the Executive Committee of Vice-Presidents, representing the economic interests at play in the integration process in each of the countries. It works closely with the central bank presidents, the ministers of finance, the sectoral councils, and the regional institutions (SIECA, CABEI, CMCA, and ECLAC), which constitute its Interinstitutional Technical Secretariat.

51. Ratification by Costa Rica is the remaining step for establishing the Central American Parliament. National elections in each of the five countries must then take place for it to proceed.

52. See Chapter 6 for a more in-depth discussion of the verification mechanisms.

53. This section relies on five special papers commissioned for this report: (1) *Situation and Perspectives of Central American Integration*, by Arturo Montenegro, México, April 1988; (2) *Priority Projects and Sectoral Programs for Central American Integration*, by Alfredo Guerra Borges, México, April 1988; (3) *Peace, Reconstruction, Development, and Democracy: The Potential of Non-Governmental Organizations*, by Eric Holt-Gimenez, CRIES-Managua, May 1988; (4) *The Potential of Political Parties*, by Joseph Eldridge, Honduras, May 1988; and (5) *Central American*

Integration: Institutions and Initiatives, IRELA-Madrid, June 1988. It also draws extensively from the Study Task Force paper by Eduardo Lizano, "Prospects for Regional Economic Integration," in the companion volume, *Central American Recovery and Development*.

54. Although Costa Rica, El Salvador, Guatemala, Honduras and Nicaragua are the historic republics of Central America, Belize and Panamá are key neighbors within the isthmus. The proximity and shared resource systems that make regional integration attractive within the five-country region also hold for incorporating Belize and Panamá. Though the special relationships that Belize and Panamá have had with the United Kingdom and the United States, respectively, have created distinctive economic systems and trade patterns, some degree of broader economic cooperation is highly desirable. Some ties with Panamá already exist in the form of regional cooperation programs (CSUCA, ICAP, IICA, CADESCA, among others) and in the form of joint sectoral programs (including energy, health, and transportation).

55. Incentives to incorporate Honduras back into the integration scheme might include the opening of markets of surplus countries to Honduran products without requiring full reciprocity for a certain period of time. If Honduras continued to experience a trade deficit, a financing mechanism could be sought whereby the surplus countries would use part of their surplus to finance productive projects in the Honduran economy.

56. A regional communications agency should be established with offices in each country of the Central American isthmus to facilitate the flow of prompt and objective information on regional trade, in accordance with the proposals made by CSUCA.

57. The Central American Common Market Fund could serve as the mechanism for carrying out this program.

58. One of the programs that could contribute most to improving the prospects of Central America is that prepared jointly by SIECA, CABEI, and ICAITI to reactivate and transform the industrial sector through reinvestments in firms that can contribute to the effort to increase exports to third countries, complement Central American production, and increase intra-regional trade.

59. Twenty-eight agricultural projects, identified in the same Plan for Immediate Action, deserve high priority. CABEI has initiated studies of some of them, including regional programs for improved seeds and production of animal and vegetable oils, as well as the regional agro-industries program. Special attention is being placed on the group of projects contained in the "preliminary program for technical cooperation to support the agricultural sector in Central America," undertaken by SIECA and CABEI with the assistance of the UNDP. Feasibility studies must be done, and a regional agricultural development policy must be developed to coordinate the different projects, building on the work already done, and making use of assistance from the international community.

60. For example, the Superior University Council of Central America (CSUCA), instrumental in developing a Central American body of thought concerning integration and development poli-

cies, was later supplemented with ICAP, the Central American Institute for Public Administration, for training upper-level administrative personnel. The Central American Institute for Research and Industrial Technology (ICAITI) was established to adapt and transfer new technologies.

As another example, CABEI established the Central American Common Market Fund in 1981 to finance the deficits arising from intra-regional trade. In 1984 the regional institutions prepared a plan for reactivating the CACM, and in 1986 the Central American Monetary Council created the DICA (Central American Import Rights) as a financial instrument to foster intra-regional trade.

61. For example, there is a Plan for Upgrading and Expanding the Central American Highway Network, requiring $1.2 billion in external financing; a CABEI proposal (within the UN Special Plan) for the Highway Reconstruction Program; a Program of Access Roads to Productive Zones for rural areas; and plans for $60 million of railroad improvements. A mammoth regional electricity plan was proposed in 1986 to expand capacity that otherwise will be exhausted by the mid-1990s, with a total investment of $5.9 billion. The Regional Telecommunications Artery also requires drastic renovation.

62. The Santo Domingo Agreement outlines payment agreements providing lines of credit for trade among the Latin American ALADI countries. Central America is currently negotiating to join the agreements.

63. Since 1983 there have been multilateral contacts with the European Economic Community, which could be extended to the debt negotiations with the Paris Club and to assistance from Latin America.

64. Unilaterally established by the United States in 1984, the CBI allows the U.S. president to grant trade concessions for exports from designated countries and to promote U.S. private investment in the region.

65. Other assumptions and the projection methodology are reviewed in Appendix 2.

Appendix 1

Immediate Action Plan Tables

Table 1. Estimates of Displaced Persons and Refugees Likely to
Return to Places of Origin

Country	Internally displaced persons	Registered refugees	Non-registered refugees	Estimated returnees*			
				ID**	RR	NRR	Total
El Salvador	500,000	30,900	295,000	200,000 (40%)	18,540 (60%)	29,500 (10%)	250,000
Guatemala	180,000	47,000	80,000	45,000 (25%)	28,000 (60%)	40,000 (50%)	113,000
Nicaragua	300,000	50,700	100,300	180,000 (60%)	30,000 (60%)	10,000 (10%)	220,000
Honduras	35,000			35,000 (100%)			35,000
Totals	1,015,000	128,600	475,300	460,000	76,540	79,500	618,000

Source: The figures are drawn from PAHO, *Plan for Priority Health Needs in Central America and Panama (PPS/CAP): Subregional Project*, Washington, D.C., July 1983.

*The estimates are calculated on the basis of different interviews with refugees and displaced persons of different nationalities. The numbers in parentheses indicate the approximate percentages of those who are likely to return.

**ID = Internally Displaced
NRR = Nonregistered Refugees
RR = Registered Refugees

Table 2. Summary of the Target Population (by priority group)

Priority Groups of Target Population	Number of People in Each Group
(1) Displaced persons and refugees likely to return to their original rural communities	618,000
(2) Those people in extreme poverty in the rural communities where group (1) resettles	463,000
(3) Displaced persons and refugees who have already resettled into new, mostly urban communities and who are not likely to return to their original rural communities	680,000
(4) Those people in the most extreme poverty in the urban communities where group (3) has resettled	510,000
Total Target Population	2,271,000

Table 3. Estimates of Biologically Vulnerable Population, in 1990 (in thousands of people)

Country	Children under 4 years old	Percentage of TP*	Adults over 60	Percentage of TP	Women 15-49 years**	Percentage of TP	Total	Percentage of TP
Costa Rica	463	15.7	185	6.3	749	25.5	1,397	47.6
El Salvador	1,264	19.5	349	5.4	1,490	23.0	3,103	47.9
Guatemala	1,900	20.7	467	3.1	2,029	22.1	4,396	47.8
Honduras	1,021	20.0	242	4.7	1,154	22.6	2,417	47.8
Nicaragua	816	21.1	167	4.3	882	22.8	1,865	48.2
	5,464		1,410		6,304		13,178	

Source: United Nations. *World Population Prospects* (Estimates and Projections as Assessed in 1984), Population Studies No. 98, (New York, 1986).

*Percentage of total population.

**All women between the ages of 15 and 49 who are nursing or pregnant.

Table 4. Cumulative Coverage of Assistance Programs (for three-year period)

Population Group*	Direct food[1] assistance	Other food[2] assistance	Supplementary food[3]	Entire package
Minimum Group Targeted for Immediate Actions (Resettlement: 2,271,500 people)	$ 411m	$1,040m	($137m)	$ 2,550m
Remaining Biologically Vulnerable in Extreme Poverty [food assistance only for additional 3,709,680 beneficiaries] (total of 6,078,000)	$1,100m	**	($464m)	$ 4,114m
Remaining Biologically Vulnerable in Extreme Poverty [full benefits for 6,078,000]	$1,100m	$2,784m	($464m)	$ 7,050m
All Those in Extreme Poverty (10,000,000)	$1,811m	$4,540m	($601m)	$11,250m

*The minimum targeted population is those refugees and displaced persons likely to return to their places of origin, plus the extremely poor in the communities where these people will resettle. The second group includes all of the targeted population plus all biologically vulnerable people in extreme poverty (48% of 7,728,500). We extend only direct food assistance to the additional biologically vulnerable people. The fourth group, including all those in extreme poverty, is calculated from a total estimated population of 10 million people living in extreme poverty (from CEPAL) minus those already addressed as the minimum targeted population.

**This group does not receive Other Food Assistance.

[1] Direct provision of food.

[2] Includes all other elements of food assistance, chiefly employment-generating projects. We do not assume the biologically vulnerable will take part in these work projects.

[3] Supplementary food provided only to the biologically vulnerable. See programs under Health and Nutrition.

Table 5. Distribution of Benefits (by country, for groups outlined in table 4)*

Country	Minimum Group	Remaining B.V. (food only) (percentages)	Remaining B.V. (all benefits)	All Extremely Poor
Guatemala	19	23	27	28
Nicaragua	26	21	16	13
El Salvador	42	36	29	26
Honduras	5	14	24	28
Costa Rica	8	6	5	4

*This table shows how benefits from four levels of the immediate action plan will be distributed by country. The variations in each country's benefits are due to the numbers of displaced persons and refugees within their borders and the national extent of extreme poverty.

Table 6. Cost Estimates for the Immediate Action Plan (millions of U.S. dollars)

Priority Areas	Criteria for Cost Estimates	YR1	YR2	YR3	Total
Food Security					
Rural Food Provision	Requirements estimated by family, using INCAP data The cost of the basic food basket for a family of five is $4.30 per day Provides 66% of the daily caloric requirement for one year	66.3	88.3	66.3	220.9
	Logistical and technical support (20% of food costs)	13.3	17.7	13.3	44.3
Urban Food Provision	Estimate based on one-third of families' minimal needs during one year	24.3	48.7	48.7	121.7
	Logistical and technical support (20% of food costs)	4.9	9.7	9.7	24.3
Financial Resources	Estimated $1,000 for typical loan 85% of the relocated/repatriated population will need loans Funds of $120,000 to be established for each community	97.2	129.6	97.2	324.0
Food for Work	$97,000 for each rural community Estimate based on two-thirds of the minimum salary for a rural family	78.7	87.5	78.7	244.9

Table 6. (continued)

Priority Areas	Criteria for Cost Estimates	Cost Estimates			
		YR1	YR2	YR3	Total
	during 18 months				
	$97,000 for each urban community	57.7	115.4	115.4	288.5
	Estimate based on three-fourths of the minimum urban salary for a family during 12 months				
	Rate: 1st year, 20% (595 communities); 2nd year, 40% (1,190 families); 3rd year, 40% (1,190 communities)				
Construction and Conservation	$10,000 per community Fund would cover only costs of materials, not labor	8.1	10.8	8.1	27.0
Food Outlets	One supply house for each 1,000 families (five communities)				
	Cost of installation: $2,000 Initial working capital: $10,000	1.4	2.9	2.9	7.2
	Logistical and technical support: 5% of initial investment and working funds	0.1	0.1	0.1	0.3
	Food and Funds	333.7	483.2	417.3	1,234.2
	Logistical and Technical Support	18.3	27.5	23.1	68.9
	Administrative Costs	50.1	72.5	62.6	185.2
Subtotal Food Security		402.1	583.2	503.0	1,488.3
Health and Nutrition					
Health Posts	For repopulated rural areas, one per community; investment cost: $8,000	6.5	8.6	6.5	21.6
	For urban areas, one unit for each 20,000 inhabitants; investment cost: $250,000 each	3.0	6.0	6.0	15.0
Emergency Medical Services	Estimates for each community	3.9	5.2	3.9	13.0
	Services and medicine: 60% of the construction costs for each health center	1.8	3.6	3.6	9.0
Rehydration and Intestinal	Estimates for all children under four years old living in extreme poverty	1.1	1.1	1.1	3.3

Table 6. (continued)

| Priority Areas | Criteria for Cost Estimates | Cost Estimates | | | |
		YR1	YR2	YR3	Total
Disorders	directly related to displacement (455,000) Estimate of 70,000 children born each year Oral rehydration costs based on three bouts of diarrhea a year, at $1 per bout				
	Technical and logistical support (30% of costs)	0.5	0.5	0.5	1.5
	Parasite treatment costs based on $3 per person each year for three years	1.1	1.1	1.1	3.3
	Technical and logistical support (30% of costs)	0.5	0.5	0.5	1.5
Tropical Diseases	Estimates per community Treatment for each family: $6.50 Continuous treatment for three years	1.1	2.5	3.5	7.1
	Technical and logistical support (60% of treatment costs)	0.6	1.5	2.1	4.2
Vaccination Campaigns	Assuming that 124,000 children under four years old will return and that there will be 70,000 births a year Costs per dose: $4 Four doses in the first year	2.1	2.4	2.1	6.6
Supplementary Food Program Pregnant Women	Estimate based on the population of pregnant women (average fertility rates of over 20% in each country, or 500,000 women each year) Maintain the program for 12 months for each pregnant woman Nutritional complement according to INCAP data: 600 calories a day at an approximate cost of $38 per year	19.0	19.0	19.0	57.0

Table 6. (continued)

Priority Areas	Criteria for Cost Estimates	Cost Estimates			
		YR1	YR2	YR3	Total
Children	Children who are displaced or directly affected by the conflict: 455,000 INCAP data: food supplement of 400 calories per day at a cost of $35 each year, for three years	15.9	15.9	15.9	47.7
	Technical and logistical support (30% of direct costs for pregnant women and children)	10.5	10.5	10.5	31.5
Mental and Physical Health	Programs of mental health for communities, integrated with programs of health, nutrition, and education (10% of costs of equipment and services)	0.6	0.9	0.7	2.2
	Assumes an injured population of 20,000, at a cost of $100 per person each year	2.0	2.0	2.0	6.0
Education for Health	Assumes all health and nutrition programs have an educational component Estimates the educational component to be 2% of the cost of all programs	1.2	1.4	1.3	3.9
	Health and Nutrition Programs	59.3	69.7	66.7	195.7
	Logistical and Technical Support	12.1	13.0	13.6	38.7
	Administrative Costs	8.9	10.4	10.0	29.3
Subtotal Health and Nutrition		80.3	93.1	90.3	263.7
Drinking Water and Sanitation					
Temporary Measures	Assuming $1 per day for transporting the water from the source to the community, for wood to boil the water, and for chlorine tablets for purification Assistance will be maintained for three months, during which drinking water systems will be reestablished	8.7	11.7	8.7	29.1

Table 6. (continued)

| Priority Areas | Criteria for Cost Estimates | Cost Estimates | | | |
		YR1	YR2	YR3	Total
Provision of Drinking Water	For urban areas, augment the number of community connections in each urban location contemplated in the program. Average cost per community: $5,000	3.0	6.0	6.0	15.0
	Repair and/or construction of a drinking water system for each community at $20,000 in rural areas	16.2	21.6	16.2	54.0
Sewage and Sanitation	Estimates based on families, assuming that 60% of families in communities of 200 families are without latrines Estimated cost of a latrine is $25, which includes the septic tank, materials for walls and roof, toilet and cement slab	2.4	3.2	2.4	8.0
	Technical and logistical support (50% of costs of materials)	1.2	1.6	1.2	4.0
	Sewage tank construction for each community involved at a cost of $2,000 per community Average cost per community: $10,000	6.0	11.9	11.9	29.8
	Trash collection: four dumps per community involved at a cost of $2,000 each per month per community	1.2	2.4	2.4	6.0
	Improving municipal collection services: $250 per month per community	1.8	3.8	3.8	9.4
	Programs for Drinking Water and Sanitation	39.3	60.6	51.4	151.3
	Logistical and Technical Support	1.2	1.6	1.2	4.0
	Administrative Costs	5.9	9.1	7.7	22.7
Subtotal Drinking Water and Sanitation		46.4	71.3	60.3	178.0
Housing					
Provision of Building	$250 in building materials for each family (zinc sheets and wood)	24.3	32.4	24.3	81.0

Table 6. (continued)

Priority Areas	Criteria for Cost Estimates	Cost Estimates			
		YR1	YR2	YR3	Total
Materials	Hardware and nails: one set per family at $15/set	1.5	1.9	1.5	4.9
	Minimal equipping for housing: $35 per family	3.4	4.5	3.4	11.3
	Housing Programs	29.2	38.8	29.2	97.2
	Logistical and Technical Support	1.5	1.9	1.5	4.9
	Administrative Costs	4.4	5.9	4.4	14.7
Subtotal for Housing		35.1	46.6	35.1	116.8
Education					
School Repair and Construction	$5,000 per classroom, estimating a one-room schoolhouse for grades 1–3 for each community of 200 families	4.0	5.4	4.0	13.4
	A three-room schoolhouse for every five communities for grades 4–6	2.4	3.2	2.4	8.0
	For urban locations, estimates based on $15,000 for every five communities	1.8	3.6	3.6	9.0
Teachers and School Supplies	One teacher per classroom in rural schools, with a salary of $200/month during 12 months	3.1	4.1	3.1	10.3
	For each urban school, two teachers per classroom, contemplating two shifts (morning and evening), with a salary of $200/month for 12 months	1.7	3.4	3.4	8.5
	For rural schools, 10% of expenditures for equipment and 15% for materials	0.6	0.9	0.6	2.1
		1.0	1.3	1.0	3.3
	For urban schools, 15% of expenditures for equipment and 20% for materials	0.3	0.5	0.5	1.3
		0.4	0.7	0.7	1.8
	For rural schools, 5% of expenditures for repair and maintenance of equipment and materials during three years	0.2	0.3	0.2	0.7
	For urban schools, 10% of expenditures for repair and	0.2	0.4	0.4	1.0

Table 6. (continued)

| Priority Areas | Criteria for Cost Estimates | Cost Estimates | | | |
		YR1	YR2	YR3	Total
	maintenance of equipment and materials during three years				
Literacy Programs	Programs to be developed by community, with an emphasis on	0.8	1.1	0.8	2.7
	female heads of households in urban areas (percentage of coverage: 80% of adult women, 60% of adult men) Cost per person per year: $6 for first year, $3 for second year, and 2$ for third year Using illiteracy rate of 75% for women and 60% for men	0.6	1.2	1.2	3.0
	Technical and logistical support (20% of estimated costs)	0.2	0.2	0.2	0.6
		0.1	0.2	0.2	0.5
Technical Training Agricultural	For rural areas, directed at one adult per family Demonstration lots, on-site training, follow-up and reinforcement during two farm cycles: $200 per person in first year; $100 per person per year in second and third years	38.8	51.8	38.8	129.4
Construction and Conservation	For rural communities, directed at adult members of families Promoting technicians, travel allowances, educational materials. One promoter for every five communities at an annual cost of $3,000 (salaries, travel allowances, and materials)	0.5	0.6	0.5	1.6
	Education Programs	56.4	78.5	61.2	196.1
	Logistical and Technical Support	3.1	4.3	3.5	10.9
	Administrative Costs	8.4	11.8	9.2	29.4
Subtotal for Education		67.9	94.6	73.9	236.4

Table 6. (continued)

Priority Areas	Criteria for Cost Estimates	Cost Estimates			
		YR1	YR2	YR3	Total
Fundamental Rights					
Securing Documentation	80% of the assisted rural population needs documentation, and 40% of the	0.4	0.5	0.4	1.3
	assisted urban population finds themselves in similar circumstances Assumes the cost of documentation per individual in rural areas is $1.50, and $1.00 for urban areas and that the documentation process can be done by local officials	0.2	0.4	0.4	1.0
Land and Property Rights	Assumes that the cost of title is 1% of the property value. Assumes the average value of each 1.75 acres is $1,000 Assumes that the total number of acres to be titled is 700	3.2	4.3	3.2	10.7
Urban Living Security	Assumes that legal services are $10/ family The problem should be approached from a community level	0.7	1.4	1.4	3.5
Organizational Programs	Costs are estimated by community, accumulated during three years	2.0	4.7	6.8	13.5
	$2,500 per rural community; $2,000 per urban community	1.2	3.6	6.0	10.8
	Programs for Fundamental Rights	7.7	14.9	18.2	40.8
	Logistical and Technical Support	0.4	0.7	0.9	2.0
	Administrative Costs	1.3	2.2	2.8	6.3
Subtotal Fundamental Rights		9.4	17.8	21.9	49.1
Physical Infrastructure					
Reconstruction of Services	Fund of $10,000 per community Labor is financed through food for	8.1	10.8	8.1	27.0

Table 6. (continued)

| Priority Areas | Criteria for Cost Estimates | Cost Estimates | | | |
		YR1	YR2	YR3	Total
	work program				
	Costs include only construction				
	materials and other direct costs				
Reconstruction of Roadways	Repair costs estimated at $300 per KM Assumes the average distance of the communities from the closest access road is 20KM	4.9	6.5	4.9	16.3
Electrical Power	Gasoline generators during the period in which the system is being repaired or initiated: $3,800 per generator;	2.9	1.0	0.0	3.9
	$1.50 per gallon of gasoline, one gallon daily for six months	0.2	0.3	0.2	0.7
	200 home connections per community at $50 per connection, 15,000 meters of wire at $2 per linear meter, 150 posts at $10 per post, and three transformers at $200 per transformer	34.1	45.5	34.1	113.7
Communications Systems	Repair of the physical plants at a cost of $2,000 Installation/repair of equipment: $5,000 per system	5.7	7.6	5.7	19.0
	Program for Reconstruction of Physical Infrastructure	55.9	71.7	53.0	180.6
	Logistical and Technical Support	2.8	3.6	2.6	9.0
	Administrative Costs	8.3	10.8	7.9	27.0
Subtotal for Reconstruction of Physical Infrastructure		67.0	86.1	63.5	216.6
Total for All Programs		581.5	817.4	697.0	2,095.9
Logistical and Technical Support		39.4	52.6	46.4	138.4
Administrative Costs (15%)		87.3	122.1	103.8	313.2
Total for the Entire Plan		708.2	992.1	847.2	2,547.5

Appendix 2

Capital Requirements

In order to derive estimates of capital inflows required by countries of the region to sustain increased imports, projections were made of the balance of payments. Table 1 indicates the principal assumptions used. A key element is the income growth trajectory projected for the countries over the period 1989–93. Two alternative scenarios are specified: one with, and the other without, debt service reduction. Debt reduction lowers payments on current debt to private creditors; this could occur through debt write-down or capitalization with a grace period for principal repayment. For Nicaragua, the relief must be greater and is reflected here by a write-down of official debt by three-fourths and private debt by 90 percent. For Costa Rica, the write-down is 50 percent.

The assumptions imply a continuing commitment to nontraditional exports as well as some revival of traditional ones; prices over the period are forecast as slightly unfavorable, reflected in modest further losses in the terms of trade. Imports are assumed to expand proportionally with production, possibly understating needs in a period of renewed growth, but intended to reflect opportunities for efficient domestic production of import substitutes. There is also allowance for import of inputs for increased production of nontraditional exports.

Table 2 indicates the implications for required net capital inflows over the five-year period by country under the two debt scenarios. Gross requirements would add in scheduled (and potentially rescheduled) amortization of the debt, but are excluded here to focus on the net magnitudes.

With debt restructuring, essential to improving the prospects of Costa Rica and Nicaragua, annual net inflows of the order of $2 billion permit gradual recuperation to a sustainable growth path of 5.5 percent by 1993. In the absence of new debt arrangements, the bill would mount by an additional $500 million annually to keep pace with scheduled interest payments. The largest per capita requirements correspond to Nicaragua, given its very low level of exports, and to Honduras and El Salvador. The impact of conflict is clear.

Import growth at a 1 percent higher annual rate of increase raises capital requirements by about $200 million a year. A shortfall in exports of 1 percent from the initial assumptions would cause an increase in capital requirements of slightly less than $200 million per year. Conversely, improved export performance would reduce requirements by about the same degree.

Tables 3 to 9 provide detailed country information. Several conclusions may be highlighted here. In the first instance, recovery is unable to restore 1980 income per capita levels except in Costa Rica; El Salvador and Nicaragua lag much further behind. Second, trade deficits remain much too high not only in these two countries, but also in the others. Even reasonable export growth cannot be expected to erase the need to finance imports. But better export performance is essential. This explains the emphasis in the strategy upon realistic exchange rates and increased investments that show competitiveness in world markets as well as regional markets. Additional capital inflows will be needed after 1993, as will a significant effort to reduce their importance in total finance.

Third, with the growth in investment ratios to higher levels, domestic savings rates must also increase even while capital inflows continue. Ways must be found to stimulate savings; one important potential source is the public sector. Thus a major internal effort is the counterpart to more effectively deployed external assistance.

The approximately $2 billion estimated level of required inflow compares with net official flows of about $1 billion a year from all donors to the region, excluding Nicaragua from 1983–87. The financing of the current account deficit in that country adds another $500 million in recent years. The recommended capital flow in the report does not much exceed present magnitudes, although clearly it will have to be applied in a way that achieves more favorable results. It is also true that the sources of Nicaraguan assistance would change, placing greater demands upon the United States and the other industrialized countries as well as the multilateral institutions.

Our projections are lower than the estimates made by the Kissinger Commission, which originally called for a combined inflow of private and public capital of $20.8 billion over the period of 1984–90 for the five countries. That much higher level assumed private loans and investments of a quarter of the total. Such participation of private sources is unrealistic for the immediate future. As a consequence, our economic performance targets are correspondingly lower.

The calculations here put stress upon debt restructuring as a necessity. Without reduced debt service, the needed capital inflows for Costa Rica and Nicaragua take on much higher values and lead to unsupportable levels of outstanding debt. This can be seen by reference to Tables 3 and 4 and Tables 8 and 9.

Any projections can only be approximate. Countries in the region start from weak balance-of-payments situations and are vulnerable to changes in international conditions. Adverse terms of trade have been especially costly in the 1980s. A deteriorating world economy would obviously complicate regional economic recovery and make these estimates an understatement. But under reasonable external circumstances, a firm commitment to resource flows of $2 billion could serve as a basis for sound recovery and sustainable development.

Table 1. Assumptions: 1989–93

	CR	ES	G	H	N
Export Volume (%)	7.2	5.7	6.8	6.2	13.0
Traditional	4.2	5.6	3.2	6.4	17.1
Nontraditional	9.8	5.8	10.3	5.7	3.9
Import elasticity[a]	1	1	1	1	1
Terms of trade (%)	−.4	−.4	−.4	−2.3	−.4
International Inflation (%)	5.0	5.0	5.0	5.0	5.0
Interest Rate (%)					
Official	6.0	6.0	6.0	6.0	6.0
Private	9.0	9.0	9.0	9.0	9.0
Share of Official Flows in Transfers	.4	.8	.4	.6	.9

[a] Additional small adjustment made depending upon relative growth of nontraditional exports and assumed imported component

Table 2. Net Capital Requirements, 1989–93 (bill. U.S. Dollars)

	No Debt Relief			Debt Relief[a]	
	Base Scenario	Higher Income[b] Growth	Higher Export[b] Growth	Base Scenario	
Costa Rica	1.1	1.3	.8	.7	(.6)[c]
El Salvador	1.7	1.9	1.5	1.7	(1.4)[c]
Guatemala	1.8	2.1	1.6	1.7	(1.5)[c]
Honduras	1.9	2.1	1.7	1.8	(1.5)[c]
Nicaragua	6.0	6.1	5.9	4.2	(3.6)[c]
Total	12.5	13.5	11.5	10.1	(8.6)[c]

[a] Debt relief is defined as a reduction of 90 percent of Nicaraguan official private debt and 75 percent of official public debt, and for other countries capitalization of half-interest due on official private debt

[b] 1 percentage point

[c] 1988 constant dollars

Table 3. Costa Rica Basic Scenario (millions of U.S. dollars)

	1988	1989	1990	1991	1992	1993
Exports	1,238	1,448	1,586	1,768	1,960	2,163
Traditional	597	685	700	751	806	862
Nontraditional	641	763	886	1,017	1,154	1,301
Imports	1,400	1,558	1,738	1,940	2,153	2,396
Nonfactor Services	126	134	141	150	159	168
Net Interest Payments	314	323	330	338	347	356
Private Transfers	39	40	42	45	47	49
Current Account	312	259	298	315	334	371
Capital Account	315	291	334	356	376	419
Foreign Investment	69	75	82	91	100	111
Private Lending						
(for reserves)	3	32	36	40	43	49
Official Flows	243	185	216	225	234	260
Loans	146	111	129	135	140	156
Transfers	97	74	86	90	94	104
Change in Reserves	3	32	36	40	43	49
Rate of Growth						
Product (%)	3.0	4.0	5.0	5.0	5.0	5.5
Current Account/Y (%)	6.5	4.9	5.1	4.9	4.7	4.7
Investment/Y (%)	21.0	21.6	22.0	22.0	22.0	22.0
Public Savings/Domestic						
Savings (%)	26.0	26.0	26.0	27.0	28.0	31.0
Debt/Y	.97	.91	.86	.80	.76	.71
Debt/X	3.8	3.3	3.1	2.9	2.7	2.6

Table 4. Costa Rica Debt Relief: Writedown of 50 Percent of
Private Debt Owed by Government (millions of U.S. dollars)

	1988	1989	1990	1991	1992	1993
Exports	1,238	1,448	1,586	1,768	1,960	2,163
Traditional	597	685	700	751	806	862
Nontraditional	641	763	886	1,017	1,154	1,301
Imports	1,400	1,558	1,738	1,940	2,153	2,396
Nonfactor Services	126	134	141	150	159	168
Net Interest Payments	314	236	240	245	250	256
Private Transfers	39	40	42	45	47	49
Current Account	312	172	208	222	238	271
Capital Account	315	204	244	263	280	319
Foreign Investment	69	75	82	91	100	111
Private Lending (for reserves)	3	32	36	40	43	49
Official Flows	243	97	126	131	137	160
Loans	146	58	75	79	82	96
Transfers	97	39	50	52	55	64
Change in Reserves	3	32	36	40	43	49
Rate of Growth Product (%)	3.0	4.0	5.0	5.0	5.0	5.5
Current Account/Y (%)	6.5	3.3	3.7	3.6	3.5	3.7
Investment/Y (%)	21.0	21.6	22.0	22.0	22.0	22.0
Public Savings/Domestic Savings (%)	26.0	25.0	26.0	27.0	29.0	30.0
Debt/Y	.97	.72	.67	.63	.59	.55
Debt/X	3.8	2.6	2.5	2.3	2.1	2.0

Table 5. El Salvador (bill. U.S. dollars)

	1988	1989	1990	1991	1992	1993
Exports	609	634	700	781	881	994
Traditional	388	391	430	480	546	621
Nontraditional	221	243	270	301	335	373
Imports	1,033	1,127	1,243	1,375	1,515	1,678
Nonfactor Services	130	138	146	155	164	174
Net Interest Payments	148	151	155	159	163	168
Private Transfers	221	222	233	245	257	269
Current Account	231	285	319	353	377	409
Capital Account	242	304	342	379	405	441
Foreign Investment	0	2	6	13	22	35
Private Lending						
(for reserves)	12	19	23	27	28	33
Official Flows	231	283	313	340	354	374
Loans	46	57	63	68	70	75
Transfers	185	226	250	272	284	299
Change in Reserves	12	19	23	27	28	33
Rate of Growth						
Product (%)	1.5	4.0	5.0	5.0	5.0	5.5
Current Account/Y (%)	4.6	5.3	5.3	5.3	5.2	5.1
Investment/Y (%)	13.5	14.0	17.5	17.5	17.5	19.2
Public Savings/Domestic						
Savings (%)	3.5	7.1	8.4	11.3	14.2	15.3
Debt/Y	.46	.44	.41	.39	.37	.34
Debt/X	3.8	3.8	3.5	3.3	3.0	2.8

Table 6. Guatemala (millions of U.S. dollars)

	1988	1989	1990	1991	1992	1993
Exports	1,113	1,256	1,421	1,593	1,759	1,925
Traditional	586	631	678	725	776	828
Nontraditional	527	625	743	868	983	1,097
Imports	1,442	1,597	1,786	1,998	2,213	2,454
Nonfactor Services	23	24	26	28	29	31
Net Interest Payments	160	171	182	194	207	222
Private Transfers	75	79	82	87	91	95
Current Account	391	408	438	485	541	625
Capital Account	386	439	476	527	584	673
Foreign Investment	96	105	116	128	141	156
Private Lending						
(for reserves)	-5	31	38	42	43	48
Official Flows	295	303	332	356	400	469
Loans	177	182	193	214	240	281
Transfers	118	121	129	143	160	188
Change in Reserves	-5	31	38	42	43	48
Rate of Growth						
Product (%)	3	4	5	5	5	5.5
Current Account/Y (%)	4.2	4.0	3.9	3.9	3.9	4.1
Investment/Y (%)	13.5	14.0	17.5	17.5	17.5	19.2
Public Savings/Domestic						
Savings (%)	-.2	0	1.6	3.4	5.3	6.6
Debt/Y	.29	.29	.28	.28	.27	.27
Debt/X	2.5	2.4	2.2	2.2	2.1	2.1

Table 7. Honduras (millions of U.S. dollars)

	1988	1989	1990	1991	1992	1993
Exports	922	1,007	1,101	1,197	1,292	1,413
Traditional	648	703	760	817	874	953
Nontraditional	274	304	341	380	418	460
Imports	1,045	1,142	1,261	1,296	1,536	1,699
Nonfactor Services	0	0	0	0	0	0
Net Interest Payments	217	224	232	240	249	259
Private Transfers	17	17	18	19	20	21
Current Account	324	342	374	420	473	524
Capital Account	339	362	398	447	501	556
Foreign Investment	39	42	46	51	56	62
Private Lending						
(for reserves)	15	19	24	27	28	32
Official Flows	285	300	327	368	416	461
Loans	114	120	131	147	167	184
Transfers	171	180	196	221	250	277
Change in Reserves	15	19	24	27	28	32
Rate of Growth						
Product (%)	3	4	5	5	5	5.5
Current Account/Y (%)	7.5	7.3	7.2	7.3	7.5	7.5
Investment/Y (%)	14.7	14.8	18.5	18.5	18.5	20.4
Public Savings/Domestic						
Savings (%)	10	15	16	20	25	26
Debt/Y	.76	.73	.69	.65	.62	.60
Debt/X	3.6	3.4	3.2	3.1	3.0	2.9

Table 8. Nicaragua Basic Scenario (millions of U.S. dollars)

	1988	1989	1990	1991	1992	1993
Exports	264	305	376	447	534	604
Traditional	167	200	262	323	399	454
Nontraditional	97	105	114	124	135	150
Imports	916	999	1,100	1,215	1,336	1,479
Nonfactor Services	0	0	0	0	0	0
Net Interest Payments	116	444	451	458	465	473
Private Transfers	21	22	23	24	25	26
Current Account	747	1,116	1,151	1,201	1,242	1,321
Capital Account	748	1,133	1,172	1,225	1,266	1,350
Foreign Investment	0	2	6	13	22	35
Private Lending						
(for reserves)	1	17	20	23	24	29
Official Flows	747	1,114	1,145	1,189	1,220	1,287
Loans	75	111	115	119	122	129
Transfers	672	1,003	1,031	1,070	1,098	1,158
Change in Reserves	1	17	20	23	24	29
Rate of Growth						
Product (%)	−4	4	5	5	5	5.5
Current Account/Y (%)	37.9	51.9	48.7	45.9	43.1	41.4
Investment/Y (%)	16	18	22.5	22.5	22.5	24.8
Public Savings/Domestic						
Savings (%)	a	a	a	a	a	a
Debt/Y	3.3	3.1	2.9	2.7	2.5	2.3
Debt/X	24.9	22.0	18.2	15.6	13.4	12.1

a negative domestic saving

Table 9. Nicaragua Debt Relief: Writedown of 90 Percent of Private Debt and
75 Percent of Public Debt Owed by Government (millions of U.S. dollars)

	1988	1989	1990	1991	1992	1993
Exports	264	305	376	447	534	604
Traditional	167	200	262	323	399	454
Nontraditional	97	105	114	124	135	150
Imports	916	999	1,100	1,215	1,336	1,479
Nonfactor Services	0	0	0	0	0	0
Net Interest Payments						
Private Transfers	21	22	23	24	25	26
Current Account	747	767	800	848	886	963
Capital Account	748	783	820	871	910	992
Foreign Investment	0	2	6	13	22	35
Private Lending						
(for reserves)	1	17	20	23	24	29
Official Flows	747	765	794	834	864	929
Loans	75	76	79	83	86	93
Transfers	672	688	714	751	778	836
Change in Reserves	1	17	20	23	24	29
Rate of Growth						
Product (%)	−4	4	5	5	5	5.5
Current Account/Y (%)	37.9	35.7	33.8	32.4	30.8	30.2
Investment/Y (%)	16	18	22.5	22.5	22.5	24.8
Public Savings/Domestic						
Savings (%)	a	a	a	a	a	a
Debt/Y	3.3	.72	.69	.67	.64	.62
Debt/X	24.9	5.0	4.4	3.9	3.5	3.3

[a] negative domestic saving

Appendix 3

Esquipulas II Accords

The Presidents of the Republics of Guatemala, El Salvador, Honduras, Nicaragua and Costa Rica, meeting in Guatemala City on August 6–7, 1987, encouraged by the farsighted and steadfast desire for peace of the Contadora and the Support Groups, strengthened by the firm support of all the governments and peoples of the world, and their principal support international organizations—particularly the European Economic Community and His Holiness John Paul II—based on the Declaration of Esquipulas I, and coming together in Guatemala to discuss the peace plan presented by the Government of Costa Rica, have decided:

To meet fully the historic challenge of forging a peaceful future for Central America; to undertake the commitment to fight for peace and eliminate war; to make dialogue prevail over violence, and reason over rancor; to dedicate these efforts for peace to the youth of Central America, whose legitimate aspirations for peace, social justice, freedom and reconciliation have been frustrated for many generations; to make the Central American Parliament a symbol for the freedom, independence and reconciliation to which Central America aspires.

We ask for respect and assistance from the international community for our efforts.

We have Central American avenues for peace and development, but we need help to make them effective. We ask for an international treatment that will ensure development so the peace we seek will be lasting.

We repeat firmly that peace and development are inseparable.

We thank President Vinicio Cerezo Arevalo and the noble people of Guatemala for hosting this meeting.

The generosity of the President and people of Guatemala were decisive elements in creating the climate in which the peace agreements were adopted.

Procedure for Establishing Firm and Lasting
Peace in Central America

The governments of the Republics of Costa Rica, El Salvador, Guatemala, Honduras and Nicaragua, determined to achieve the objectives and develop the principles established in the Charter of the United Nations, the Charter of the Organization of American States, the Document of Objectives, the Message of Caraballeda for Peace, Security and Democracy in Central America, the Declaration of Guatemala, the Communique of Punta del Este, the Message of Panama, the Declaration of Esquipulas, and the draft Contadora Act for Peace and Cooperation in Central America of June 6, 1986, have agreed on the following procedures to establish firm and lasting peace in Central America.

1. National Reconciliation

   a. Dialogue

To undertake on an urgent basis, in those cases where deep divisions have occurred in society, actions for national reconciliation that will permit the participation of the people, with full guarantees in genuine democratic political processes, on the bases of justice, freedom and democracy, and to that end, to establish mechanisms that will make dialogue with opposing groups possible under the law.

To that end, the governments involved shall initiate a dialogue with all disarmed internal political opposition groups and with those that have availed themselves of amnesty.

   b. Amnesty

In each Central American country, except where the International Committee for Verification and Follow-up determines that it is not necessary, decrees for amnesty shall be issued that will establish all of the provisions to ensure inviolability of life, freedom in all of its forms, material property and safety of the persons to whom those decrees are applicable. Simultaneously with the issuance of the amnesty decrees, the irregular forces of the country concerned shall release all persons in their power.

   c. National Reconciliation Committee

To verify compliance with the commitments that the five Central American Governments undertake by signing this document, regarding amnesty, cease-fire, democratization and free elections, a National Reconciliation Committee shall be established that will have the duties of verifying the real effectiveness of the national reconciliation process, and the unrestricted respect for all the civil and political rights of Central American citizens that are guaranteed in this document. The National Reconciliation Committee shall be composed of a principal and alternate delegate representing the Executive Branch, a principal and alternate delegate suggested by the Episcopal Conference, and selected by the Government from a panel of bishops to be submitted within fifteen days after receipt of the formal invitation. This invitation shall be issued by the governments within five working days following the signature of this document. The same procedure using a panel shall be employed to select a principal and alternative representative of the legally-registered political opposition parties. The panel shall be submitted by the same deadline mentioned above. Each Central American Government shall also select as a member of that committee an outstanding citizen and an alternate for him who are not members either of the government or of the government's party.

The decision or decree establishing the National Committee shall be reported immediately to the other Central American governments.

2. Urging the Cessation of Hostilities

The governments strongly urge the countries in the area that are now undergoing attacks by irregular or insurgent groups to agree to ceasing hostilities.

The governments of those countries undertake to carry out all actions required to achieve an effective cease-fire under their constitutions.

3. Democratization

The governments undertake to encourage an authentic participatory and pluralistic democratic process involving promotion of social justice, respect for human rights, sovereignty, territorial integrity of the States, and the right of all countries to determine freely and without outside interference of any kind their economic, political and social models, and they shall take in a verifiable manner measures that are conducive to the establishment, and where necessary, the improvement of democratic, representative and pluralistic systems that guarantee the organization of political parties and effective participation of the people in decision-making and that ensure free access of holders of divergent political groups to honest periodic elections, based on the full observance of the rights of citizens.

To verify good faith in carrying out this process of democratization, it shall be understood that:

a. There shall be freedom of the press, radio and television. This complete freedom shall include opening and keeping in operation mass media for all ideological groups and operating those media without subjecting them to prior censorship.

b. There shall be total pluralism of political parties. In this regard, political groups shall have full access to the mass media, shall enjoy fully the rights of association and the right to public assembly in the unrestricted exercise of oral, written and televised publicity, and freedom of movement of the members of political parties in their efforts to win support.

c. In addition, the Central American Governments that have put in effect a state of emergency or seige (estado de excepcion, sitio o emergencia), shall lift it and shall put into effect the rule of law with full observance of all constitutional guarantees.

4. Free Elections

Having established the conditions inherent in any democracy, they shall hold free, pluralistic and honest elections. As a joint expression of the Central American countries to find reconciliation and lasting peace for their peoples, elections shall be held to select members of the Central American Parliament, whose establishment was proposed by the "Declaration of Esquipulas" of May 25, 1986.

For the above purposes, the Presidents expressed their resolve to proceed in organizing this Parliament, for which purpose the Preparatory Committee of the Central American Parliament shall conclude its deliberations and submit to the Central American Presidents the Draft Treaty thereon within 150 days. These elections shall be held simultaneously in all the countries of Central America in the first half of 1988 on a date that shall be agreed upon at the proper time by the Presidents of the Central American States.

The elections shall be monitored by the appropriate electoral bodies, and the governments concerned undertake to extend invitations to the Organization of American States, the United Nations, and the Governments of third countries to send observers to make sure that the electoral processes have been carried out in accordance with the strictest rules of equal access for all political parties to the mass media, and to ample facilities to hold public meetings and to conduct any other kind of campaign publicity.

So that the elections for members of the Central American Parliament are not held within the period indicated in this section, the constituent treaty shall be submitted to the five countries for approval or ratification.

After the elections for the Central American Parliament are held, there shall take place in each country with international observers and the same guarantees, within the deadlines set and the schedules that shall be proposed under the present political constitutions, equally free and democratic elections to select people's representatives in the municipalities, congresses and legislative assemblies, and the Presidents of the Republics.

5. Cessation of Aid to Irregular Forces or to Insurrectional Movements

The Governments of the five Central American countries shall request the Governments in and outside the region that openly or covertly provide military, logistic, financial, propaganda, manpower, armament, munitions, and equipment assistance to irregular forces or insurrectional movements, to cease such assistance, as an essential element for achieving stable and durable peace in the region.

Not included in the foregoing is assistance and the aid necessary for return to normal life of those persons who were members of such groups or forces.

In addition, irregular forces and insurgent groups operating in Central America shall be requested to refrain from receiving such assistance, in order to maintain a true Latin Americanist spirit. These requests shall be made pursuant to the provisions of the Document of Objectives regarding the elimination of the traffic in arms within or from outside the region for persons, organizations or groups that intend to destabilize the governments of the Central American countries.

6. Non-Use of Territory for Aggression Against Other States

The five countries signing this document reiterate their commitment to deny the use of their territory to, and not to provide or permit logistic military support for, persons, organizations or groups that seek to destabilize the governments of Central American countries.

7. Negotiation of Security, Verification and Limitation of Armaments

The Governments of the five Central American countries, with the participation of the Contadora Group, in the exercise of their mediation function, shall conduct negotiations on pending points of the agreement, regarding matters of security, verification and control in the Draft Act of Contadora for Peace and Cooperation in Central America.

The negotiations shall also cover measures for disarming the irregular forces that are ready to avail themselves of the amnesty decrees.

8. Refugees and Displaced Persons

The Central American Governments undertake to provide urgent relief to the flows of refugees or displaced persons that the regional crisis has caused, by furnishing protection and assistance particularly with health, education, employment and security problems, and to facilitate their repatriation, resettlement or relocation, provided that it is voluntary and is requested individually.

They also undertake to arrange assistance with the international community for Central American refugees and displaced persons, both directly under bilateral or multilateral agreements, and through the United Nations High Commissioner for Refugees (UNHCR) and other agencies and organizations.

9. Cooperation, Democracy and Freedom for Peace and Development

In the climate of freedom that democracy ensures, the Central American countries shall take decisions to accelerate development in order to achieve societies that are more egalitarian and free from poverty. Consolidation of democracy involves the establishment of an economy of wellbeing and an economic and social democracy.

To reach those objectives, the governments shall jointly make arrangements to obtain special economic assistance from the international community.

10. International Follow-up and Verification

   a. International Committee for Verification and Follow-up

An International Committee for Verification and Follow-up shall be established with the following members: the Secretaries General, or their representatives, of the Organization of American States and the United Nations, and the Foreign Ministers of Central America, the Contadora Group and the Support Group. This Committee shall have the duty of verification and follow-up on compliance with the commitments set forth in this document.

   b. Support for the Facilitation of the Mechanisms for Reconciliation and Verification and
   Follow-up

In order to strengthen the actions of the International Committee for Verification and Follow-up, the Governments of the five Central American countries shall issue declarations supporting its work.

These declarations may be endorsed by any countries interested in promoting the cause of freedom, democracy and peace in Central America.

The five governments shall provide any facilities needed for proper performance of the duties of verification and follow-up by the National Reconciliation Committee of each country and the International Committee for Verification and Follow-up.

11. Schedule of Execution of Commitments

Within fifteen days from the signature of this document, the Foreign Ministers of Central America shall meet as an Executive Committee to establish regulations, encourage and make viable the implementation of the decisions contained in this document, and organize the working committees so that, from that date, the processes shall be initiated that will lead to compliance with the commitments contracted within the deadlines stipulated, by means of consultations, negotiations or any other mechanisms considered necessary.

Within ninety days following the signature of this document, the commitments relating to amnesty, cease-fire, democratization, cessation of aid to irregular forces or to insurrectional movements, and the nonuse of territory for aggression against other countries, as defined in this document, shall enter into effect simultaneously. Within 120 days following signature of this document, the International Committee for Verification and Follow-up shall review the progress made in complying with the decisions set forth in this document.

Within 150 days, the five Central American presidents shall meet and shall receive a report for the International Committee for Verification and Follow-up and shall make the appropriate decisions thereon.

Final Provisions

The points contained in this document comprise an harmonious and indivisible whole.

Its signature involves the obligation, accepted in good faith, of complying simultaneously with the agreements made by the deadlines set. The Presidents of the five countries of Central America, with the political will to respond to our peoples' desire for peace, sign this document in the city of Guatemala, on the second day of the month of August, nineteen hundred eighty-seven.

Oscar Arias Sanchez
President of the Republic of Costa Rica

José Napoleon Duarte
President of the Republic of El Salvador

Vinicio Cerezo Arevalo
President of the Republic of Guatemala

José Azcona Hoyo
President of the Republic of Honduras

Daniel Ortega Saavedra
President of the Republic of Nicaragua

Appendix 4

Supporting Documents

The following documents and reports were prepared for deliberations of the International Commission for Central American Recovery and Development. The views expressed in these papers represent the opinions of the authors exclusively.

*Those studies set off by an opening asterisk appear in William Ascher and Ann Hubbard, eds., *Central American Recovery and Development: Task Force Report to the International Commission for Central American Recovery and Development* (Durham, N.C.: Duke University Press, 1989).

Richard Adams, "Memorandum on Relations Between Native Americans and the State in Central America," University of Texas, Austin, April 1988.

*Sergio Aguayo, "Displaced Persons and Central American Recuperation and Development."

*Gustavo Arcia, "Assessment of Rural Development in Central America."

*Colin Bradford, "Industrial Prospects for Central America: A Macroeconomic Policy Approach for Central America and the International Community for the Future (1987–1992)."

*Philip Brock, "Currency Convertibility, the Central American Clearing House, and the Revitalization of Intra-regional Trade in the Central American Common Market."

Joseph Eldridge, "The Potential of Political Parties," May 1988.

*Richard Feinberg, "Central American Debt: Genuinely Case-by-case Studies."

Joel Freedman, "Worker Participation," May 1988.

*John Freiberger, "Health Care in Central America."

Fundacion FADES, "Hacia una política de empleo en Centroamérica," April 1988.

*Claudio Gonzalez-Vega and Jeffrey Poyo, "Central American Financial Development."

Alfredo Guerra-Borges, "Proyectos prioritarios y programas sectoriales para la integración centroamericana," April 1988.

*Robert Healy, "A Reconnaissance of Conservation and Development Issues in Central America."

Eric Holt-Jimenez, "Peace, Reconstruction, Development and Democracy: The Potential of Non-Governmental Organizations." CRIES, Managua, May 1988.

Instituto de Relaciones Europeo-Latinoamericanas, "Central American Integration: Institutions and New Initiatives," Madrid, June 1988.

Glenn Jenkins and Carlos Gutierrez, "An Examination of Public Sector Finances in Central America," Harvard Institute for International Development, October 1988.

*Eduardo Lizano, "Prospects for Regional Economic Integration."

*Cassio Luiselli, "Macroeconomic Adjustment and Agricultural Reactivation in Central America."

*Richard McCall, "The Alliance for Progress: An Appraisal."

Arturo Montenegro, "Situación y perspectivas de la integración centroamericana," April 1988.

*Lars Schoultz, "The Responsiveness of Policy and Institutional Reform to Aid Conditionality."

*Alan Stoga, "Four Years Later: President Reagan's National Bipartisan Commission on Central America."

Joseph Thompson, "La educación para la participación popular en América Central," Inter-American Institute of Human Rights (IIDH), San José, Costa Rica, April 1988.

Joseph Thompson, "La participación democrática en centroamérica por medio de las instituciones," IIDH, May 1988.

*Stuart Tucker, "Trade Unshackled: Assessing the Value of the Caribbean Basin Initiative."

*Sally Yudelman, "Access and Opportunity for Women in Central America: A Challenge for Peace."

Comments

We, the undersigned members of the International Commission for Central American Recovery and Development, offer the following as a supplement to the Commission's official statement. We do not regard it as a dissent, but rather as a clarification of our own view and interpretation of the Commission's findings. Our supplementary statement is not incompatible with the Commission report, but is nonetheless quite different in tone.

Above all, we emphasize the importance of good economic policy and of self-help in each of the countries of the region. We likewise point out that regional integration is not to be sought for its own sake, but only for the purposes in which the costs are amply exceeded by the benefits perceived by the participating national economies and societies.

In the same vein, we believe that the rewards to good policy in each single country could be extremely high, even if new efforts to extend the integration process were for one or another reason aborted.

We also call attention to the fact that the political and military conflicts that have plagued the region have brought with them a flight of capital that it is essential to reverse in order to establish a basis for sound economic growth. No policy that is strongly redistributive in nature is compatible with the high rates of return needed to accomplish this reversal in the face of the risks that investors now perceive. Policies directed at poverty must accordingly emphasize, rather than redistribution *per se*, the productive employment of labor, the building of human capital through education and training, and the humanitarian concern for meeting minimum basic needs in the areas of health and nutrition.

Besides achieving peace and strengthening democracy, the most pressing need for the recovery and development of Central America is the exercise of courageous leadership in economic policy by the political authorities in each country. They must face unpleasant, even bitter, realities without flinching and at the same time should build a framework of economic policies within which a healthy and self-sustained growth process may take root.

While each of the other dimensions examined by the Commission has its own importance, we want to stress the internal economic policy to enhance or to impede the process of recovery and development. For example, we feel quite confident that in each single country, a set of bad economic policies can lead to zero or negative growth, while a good policy package should be capable of producing growth rates of four or five percent per year in real terms.

On the whole, good economic policy means having a sound tax system, avoiding waste in government spending, and setting clear and sensible rules of the game, within which private initiative and market forces are mobilized as key elements of the growth process. At the same time, it means keeping the fires of inflation in check, and placing manageable limits on government indebtedness both at home and abroad. It means promoting flexibility and adaptability in the markets for goods and services as well as for labor and capital. And finally, most difficult of all, it means developing confidence that a good policy framework, once achieved, will be maintained. Such confidence is needed for economic agents to be adequately motivated to take a long-term view in making investment decisions.

Arnold Harberger
Irma Acosta de Fortín
Francisco Mayorga
Roberto Murray Meza
Francisco de Paula Gutiérrez
Enrique Dreyfus
Glenn Jenkins

1. In order to have significant impact upon our major audience, namely the incoming U.S. administration and public opinion in the Central American countries, the report should have been more direct in addressing the question of what will make the countries adhere to the two key Principles of Esquipulas, namely non-intervention and democracy. There has to be an incentive (economic assistance) and a deterrent (isolation) to make participants want to follow Esquipulas. Although other countries have problems also, not to emphasize whether and how Nicaragua's government is to follow Esquipulas, Nicaragua diminishes the impact of our report.

2. The report endorses the idea of countries repurchasing their bank debts. Other options should be mentioned. Why should scarce aid from Northern European countries—the possible source of funding for the debt repurchase—be used to pay back amortization *in advance* when there are huge needs for high priority assistance well identified in the report. There are other ways in which the big discounts on bank debt can be translated into much-needed relief for debtors (to cite a few: Senator Bradley's proposals, or my own published proposal).

3. The report should be more forthright on the subject of State Enterprises. The idea of "Principios Orientadores" is too vague in my view. Even though state enterprises are not numerous, the idea of privatization should have been more clearly endorsed. It China and Hungary are privatizing, so should Central America.

Pedro-Pablo Kuczynski

Within the objectivity and equanimity of the report, several positive aspects of the military remain unmentioned. In Guatemala, for instance, the military has used the opportunity of the opening to support the process of democratization of the country.

In the task of searching for peace, democracy and economic and social development, all sectors and institutions in Central America are committed, in the spirit of unity and solidarity, within which there is room only for peaceful and concerted solutions.

Federico Linares

As this report suggests, large-scale external assistance will be necessary to promote recovery and establish the basis for sustained economic and social development in Central America. It should be noted that the amount called for, $2 billion per year for the next five years, is similar in magnitude to that recommended earlier by the Kissinger Commission. The report, however, may underestimate the difficulties involved in making such a large sum available. This will be a significant challenge for the international community, particularly at a time when needs are so great in many other parts of the world.

Sol Linowitz

Library of Congress Cataloging-in-Publication Data
International Commission for Central American Recovery and
Development.
The report of the International Commission for Central American
Recovery and Development : poverty, conflict, and hope / by
International Commission for Central American Recovery and
Development.
p.   cm.
Includes index.
ISBN 0-8223-0897-5.—ISBN 0-8223-0933-5 (pbk.)
1. Central America—Economic policy.   2. Central America—Social
policy.   3. Political participation—Central America.   4. Central
America—Economic integration.   5. Marginality, Social—Central
America.   I. Title.   II. Title: Poverty, conflict, and hope.
HC141.I597   1989
338.9728—DC20   89-1475